THE OFFICIAL INSIDE STORY

Siân Solanas

CARLTON
BOOKS

This is a Carlton book

First published in Great Britain in 2002 by

Carlton Books Limited
20 Mortimer Street
London W1T 3JW

Photographs by Jeff Spicer, Brian Ritchie, Tony Russell, Mark Ellis

A catalogue record for this book is available from the British Library.

ISBN 1 84222 536 7

Printed and bound in Britain by Butler & Tanner Ltd,
Frome and London

Project Editor: Lorna Russell
Senior Designer: Vicky Holmes
Designer: Anita Roddells
Jacket Designer: Alison Tutton
Production: Garry Lewis and Janette Burgin

The publishers would like to thank
Pat Smith at Carlton Pictures for all his help.

Contents

FOREWORD
by Simon Cowell

Hello

As Pete Waterman put it, welcome to the auditions from hell. It's been a marathon, and at the end of all this, I don't think I've ever felt that I've needed a holiday so much in my life. It has been an emotional rollercoaster all the way, but 90 per cent of it has been fantastic. It's gone beyond our wildest dreams, and in some ways been a life-changing experience… mainly for the good.

I would suggest to anyone who wants a career in the music industry to read this book and watch this show back. I think if you can see it from my point of view and the artists', it's the most accurate assessment of how the music industry really is: the instant high and sometimes the massive low that comes after a performance. It's all here – the competitiveness, the camaraderie, the bickering, the full-scale arguments, the jealousy. Everything has been thrown into this programme and at points it felt like a real-life soap opera rather than a talent competition.

I feel incredibly proud of what *Pop Idol* has done. When I looked at the final five for the first time in the cold light of day, I thought, "Bingo!" We had absolutely the right result.

There's Darius, a Lazarus who came back from the dead. He was the laughing stock of the nation and now he's in the top five of the biggest talent search ever. Hayley's there simply because she has an amazing voice. Then there's Zoe – the most confident 16-year-old I've ever met in my life, who remained smiling throughout. Will is a middle-class boy who had very bad early auditions but then answered me back – and just got stronger and stronger after that. Then you have Gareth, whose story is like something out of a Hollywood film: the boy who has a vocal disability and has been bullied all his life because of it and is sometimes too nervous to speak in public… yet he gets up in front of ten million people every week and sings his heart out. You couldn't have designed that, and that's what we ended up with, all because you voted them there.

This great book delves into all the emotions and goes behind the scenes on the programme that has without question been the most accurate insight into the music industry ever. Read about the squabbles, the fun, the laughing, the humiliation and the rejection – from the hilarious first auditions to the gripping final showdown. Just don't mention the high-waisted trousers…

Simon

Auditions

The atmosphere is electric. Pete Waterman is telling a story about Ferraris, Declan Donnelly is munching on a banana, Simon Cowell is polishing his teeth. Welcome to London, during the biggest auditions the world has ever seen, to create the nation's next Pop Idol. A competition that spans the length and breadth of the country, it has seen 10,000 people apply and has entranced pop fans and pop grans alike. For, from 10,000, 9,999 must be rejected as YOU decide who the Pop Idol will be in a series of oh-so-simple telephone votes. The power! The ease! The glamour! It's almost impossible to believe the excitement that such a show can conjure up.

Yet at the auditions, it's well tense. Boys and girls are falling over themselves with nerves. Some sing to themselves, others make new friends, some merely sit and look… misty. For most, this is an opportunity that they can't afford to mess up.

PRESENT AT THE AUDITIONS ARE, IN NO PARTICULAR ORDER:

* The auditionees – loads of them, sitting around, waiting their turn. The auditions are staggered, so people are told to arrive at different times – can't have 10,000 people all waiting at once, can we? The auditions take place in London, Manchester and Glasgow. People have travelled miles and woken up very early indeed to get here.

* The judges – Nicki Chapman, Simon Cowell, Pete Waterman and Neil 'Dr' Fox (Foxy). They sit behind a desk and look scary.

* The presenters – loveable Geordie tykes Ant and Dec, who have to cheer the winners and console the losers. "Some of the kids come out, and they're so upset!" says Ant, all sympathy. "They say 'Oh, I know I didn't do myself justice, I should have sung this song or that song,' and I think, 'Well, you should have done, then, shouldn't you?'" Oh Ant, you are mean.

Just what is a
pop idol?

This is a tricky one. None of the judges can put their finger on it.

Foxy: "We're trying to find someone unique, so we can hear a voice and say we haven't heard that voice before. The winner of this will not be a clone - they won't sound like Ronan or Robbie or Anastacia or Britney. It's hard to find someone with the X-factor, that thing, but when we see it we're all agreeing that there's something there we like and that we want to see more of."

Nicki: "Often people give you the lines 'I'm really funny' or 'I've always wanted to do this'. That's dull, we've all heard it a million times. It's the people that you want to sit next to at a dinner party – not the loudest people, but when there's something about them. Sometimes the quietest people are the most interesting. The dinner-party test is a great test."

Simon: "It's going to be bloody hard finding the right people. I see around 400 artists a year and only sign one or two of them. At the end of the day, you've either got star quality or you haven't. It's not something you can fake or make."

Pete: "I can't bear over-confidence. I always think that people are cocky to cover up the fact that they have no talent."

So... it's about the X-factor.

A *je ne sais quoi.*

That extra zing!

So just who are
the judges?

PETE WATERMAN
– HE'S GOT THE POPOLOGY

Mr Waterman has had 21 Number Ones, 200 Top Tens, and sold over 500 million records as producer for the likes of Kylie, Rick Astley, Bananarama, Mel and Kim, Steps and Westlife. He knows everything there is to know about pop, and has a tree growing inside his house. He is, of course, plain-speaking, no-nonsense Uncle Pete from The North, and if he don't like you, he don't like you – whether you plead with him or threaten to take him outside (see auditions section). Pete is mean.

Pete: "Hey! Did you say I was mean? [Huffs a bit.] You can't be soft when you say to someone 'no' – because no is no. The Japanese don't have a word for 'no', because it's offensive. We're here, being offensive. That's the way it is."

Gulp. He continues, "People think there are hundreds of Robbie Williamses around, but someone like him is one in 25,000. It's a bit like looking for a needle in a haystack. We're four pop professors here. It's popology."

SIMON COWELL
HE HAS EXCEPTIONALLY BRIGHT TEETH

Simon Cowell is head of the A&R department at the fantastic BMG Records, and he's signed such luminaries as Westlife and Five. He has very bright teeth and drives a posh car. Simon is excited at the prospect of helping the search for the nation's new Pop Idol, but he's no easy guy to impress, oh no.

"Listen," he says, glaring. "It's very simple. I'm at the auditions and I choose someone based on whether I'd choose them under normal circumstances. With the winner I would invest close on three to four million quid over a year. That's what's gonna be spent on this person, so they have to be stunning.

"Entrants must rehearse, rehearse and rehearse. It's important they go to the audition and do the best they can do. They've only got one chance."

NICKI CHAPMAN
SHE'S A NICE LADY

> **"Do you have another song you can sing for us?"**

Starting as a publicist, Nicki's worked with Take That, M People and the Spice Girls. She now works with Simon Fuller at 19 Management and has looked after the likes of S Club 7 and Billie. She's eager to look at all the candidates and make her thoughts known in that calm, diplomatic Nicki Chapman way, as 19 will be looking after the *Pop Idol* winner. Nicki is the soul of decency, who always finds something positive to say about each one of the hopefuls – quite a tricky job, under the circumstances.

"We've all been fair, I think," she says, soothingly. **"I know how tough it's going to be, but the only way to impress us is by enjoying the audition. We're looking for a star, not a wallflower.** I'm not saying they have to be the loudest person or the most outgoing, but they need to have a quiet confidence that will see them through."

And on Pete's dramatic judging style: "I wouldn't like anyone to think Pete's come here with the idea that he's going to be the opinionated one, that he's going to hack everybody off. Pete's being very honest with everybody, and Pete's time is money. Perhaps Foxy and I are being a bit more diplomatic, which you shouldn't always be at an audition."

DR FOX
HE'S NOT A REAL DOCTOR

He presents the Pepsi Chart, he hosts the drivetime show on London's Capital Radio and he's here, dressed in shirts so loud they would make Lily Savage blush, as a judge for *Pop Idol*. Foxy, who drives a big motorbike and likes chocolate, plays pop music all the time, so he should know what to look out for. He's adamant he doesn't want to hear anyone who sounds like anyone else, but he's quite nice to the auditionees, as he knows how nerve-wracking the process must be.

"All the finalists are being given a great opportunity as ITV prime time is the TV equivalent of playing Wembley Stadium," says Foxy. "I'm sure that every agent in the country will be tuning in to see what talent we've discovered. The nice thing is it's ultimately up to the public vote.

"I think if I had to give myself a nickname, I'd like to give myself the nickname Fair Foxy. I want to be fair. It's not about being nasty with people, it's about being honest with them. If I really think they haven't got any talent then I won't say, 'No, you're useless, goodbye, you're no use to anyone.' I want to say, 'This is a weakness – I don't think you've got the greatest voice, or whatever.'"

> **"Don't listen to Pete, I quite liked it."**

ANT AND DEC

Formerly the dynamic pop duo PJ & Duncan, Ant and Dec have witnessed the pop lifestyle close up, and know the joys and the pain of living in the spotlight. With 14 hits under their belts including the top-ten hit "Let's Get Ready To Rumble", they managed to release three albums which went platinum.

Says Ant, "Dec did all the singing. I just did some of the raps."

Says Dec, "We had a great time but it was very hard work."

Ant and Dec quit pop to become TV presenters and are best known for fronting the award-winning *SMTV:///Live* and *CD:UK* with Cat Deeley. They're renowned for their jovial style on amazingly successful shows like the *Ant and Dec Show*, *Ant and Dec Unzipped*, *Friends Like These* and *Slap Bang!* They've won two BAFTAS and countless other awards. These Geordie chaps are truly magnificent and very handsome!

"Aw, don't cry now, pet, don't cry. Oh, have me hanky now."
"It's all right, take something positive out of it."

The Hopefuls

10,000 people filled in application forms and set off for the auditions held in Glasgow, Manchester and London over a period of four weeks. For some, it was their first time auditioning; others had done the rounds. "But I auditioned for

"That Pete Waterman! He's a **!"**

"Pete, you're a bully!"

"Simon looks like a slimeball. He is a slimeball!"

Er, there was quite a lot of this.

Five!" they would cry. "No wonder you didn't get in!" Simon would reply. Out of the four judges, Nicki and Foxy were diplomatic and the auditionees liked and respected them. Simon and Pete, on the other hand, inspired complete hatred. Complete rational hatred.

Right then, who's got what it takes?

Some people, they're all ego; some are like nervous chicks shivering in the cold. However, everyone has the same goal – to convince the judges they should go through to the next round of auditions, and prove that they themselves really are the Pop Idol.

No matter how talented each youngster might be – and the standard varies enormously – everyone has a feeling they're what the judges are looking for. Everyone. No one here has any self-doubt. Some think they might have performed the wrong song or started in the wrong key, but if they don't get through to the next round they're sure they'll do it at their next audition. Some have never been at an audition before; others are seasoned auditionees who have tried out for every group going. None the less, the judges aren't interested in the amount of professional experience someone's had – all they want is confidence, a great voice and a strong image. **A Pop Idol doesn't have to be young, slim and good-looking, but they have to be stunning in some way. Take, for example, the multi-platinum artists opposite:**

MADONNA – over 40

TOM JONES – over 50

ROBBIE – hyperactive, sometimes gets a bit porky

ELTON JOHN – a bit thin on top

KYLIE – miniscule!

LIAM GALLAGHER – sings funny

The Relatives

Mums are everywhere, consoling or cheering their little ones when they come out of the dreaded audition room. Chantelle's mum is as nervous as her daughter, and they both cry when she doesn't go through. The most unusual appearance is by Elvis, i.e. Danny Gibson, who is far too old to audition… but he's here with his nephew Andy, who's a welder. Danny performs Elvis, Buddy Holly and Louis Armstrong songs around Norfolk, and will show you his false leg quite gladly.

He's gunning for Andy, who looks like someone out of Spandau Ballet (he's got dubious leather trousers on). Andy gives it a go – but fails to please the judges. He goes back to Norwich to weld with Uncle Elvis. But they'll have a few stories to tell, won't they?

Manchester

The vetting process pulls no punches and some of the auditionees don't even see the judges as they are so, er, hard on the ear that they have to be weeded out beforehand. The truth, hard to swallow, but the truth, pop friends. The auditions in Manchester, however, are extremely exuberant and there's a real feeling of exhilaration among the entrants and the panel.

The Sexual Sharman (i.e. Ben) causes a lot of excitement among fellow auditionees as he prances around beforehand. When it comes to his turn, however, his singing is just a liddle too extravagant. Pete is kind – for Pete – and says he didn't hear Sexual Sharman in the voice, just an impersonation of Westlife. This has been one of the greatest complaints by the panel – this isn't karaoke, it's not about impersonation.

Sharman puts his head in his hands, drops to the floor and cries, then moves to the wall behind, hits it fiercely and walks out.

"I thought he took it quite well," says Simon, the rotter.

Many have dressed up for the auditions but that won't always impress the judges. Kirsty puts on her pink suit for the judges and Simon is speechless. She looks like a lollipop. She gets through – her voice is good – and she's told to dress down in London.

Many who've been singing in clubs or in bands at home don't impress the judges, who still aren't sure what they're looking for but know what they don't like. Simon says, honestly, "If I had a 17-year-old pop star, 29 stone, with acne, I think we'd have a real battle on our hands."

But can he be proved wrong? The fact is, there isn't a Pop Idol template, because all sorts of different people are getting through.

Gareth Gates, 17, is a student from Bradford. He arrives at the Manchester auditions with his sister Nicola, as they usually sing together. Nicola goes in to see the judges before her brother, but they think she's too inexperienced at 16. Gareth follows, and when asked his name he is silent… Gareth has a stammer, but when he opens his mouth to sing – ah! The voice of an angel! The judges are well impressed and Gareth goes through to London.

Little Oliver, all of about three foot five, wows Pete and Nicki with his "good little pop voice", a concept which Sly Simon disagrees with, as usual. "I'd give you a job as a solo singer," says Pete. "I think you could absolutely be a pop star." Oliver grins and leaves the room.

It takes only a few hours for Pete to start railing, when he tries to ban Anastacia songs. She is clearly a big influence, but her brand of hollering is not easily mimicked. And the judges don't want to see any mimicking anyway, so that's that. When some come in to sing Elvis or The Verve it's just as bad. Sometimes, though, the judges are entertained. The girl who bravely wiggled in front of the judges as she performed a long, chirpy, quite insane version of The Village People's "YMCA" may go down in history as one of the funniest singers on the telly. Ah, but she can never be a Pop Idol though, can she? Anthony, the kickboxing champion who offered Pete out for a fight was, er, memorable too. Shall we see what happened in Glasgow?

Glasgow

Home of the deep-fried Mars Bar, would Glasgow serve up any deep-lunged singers? Well, there's a fair share of odd persons in school caps and glasses, who look more *Byker Grove* than Top 40. Some just come to get their Jason Donovan records signed, others merely want to demonstrate to Ant and Dec that they can hide 50p in their belly button.

Laura is over from Northern Ireland, and her mum is very keen. "If anyone beats Laura," she says, "that's got to be some person." Well, it would be – a person, that is. Laura wows the judges with a bit of Janet Jackson and 387 words per second. Simon asks her if she knows what a comma is – she's so nervous she hasn't paused for breath. The panel take her through to the next round.

Paul sings one of Pete's songs, "Never Gonna Give You Up" by Rick Astley, although he says he didn't know Pete had written it. Paul hops about like a hot chicken and leaps just as erratically from key to key.

"I didn't write that song! That's not the song I wrote," says Pete, with his usual candour.

Then the judges are surprised to see someone they already know the name of. Darius Danesh, he of the other pop-star competition, has turned up to the auditions (with guitar, of course). Why oh why is he putting himself through this again?

"I'm here as a challenge," he says. "There were offers before, but I didn't feel ready for recording commitments."

Darius wants to sing his own songs accompanied by his guitar, but Simon tells him "no exceptions" and he sings something by Seal.

"I don't know you, Darius," says Pete. "It's an interesting song to pick. I think you gave a great performance."

"I'd lose your corniness," says Simon. "I still think you're corny."

Ah, but he still gets through, though, doesn't he? How will he fare at the London recall auditions?

London

Thousands more step through the glowering portals of the London ExCeL centre in Docklands, hoping the judges will realise their true potential. Many people think they can get away with "forgetting" their ID, which proves their age – you have to be between 16 and 26, no younger or older. George runs to the toilet to "find" his ID when Simon asks him for it… and never comes back.

Again, many of the potential Pop Idols are vocally challenged. Howard tries to sing East 17, then rap, then breakdance. Well, he's very good at breakdancing… Lauren from Croydon got the sack this morning for bunking off work, and says her dad is going to kill her – he doesn't want her to go to auditions, he wants her to get a "proper" job. Darnit, so does Simon.

"I agree with your dad."

She's not through. Devastated, she goes home to tell Pops. Oh dear.

Rik Waller, 20, from Gillingham, Kent, is nervous, "excruciatingly nervous".

"I'm six foot three, built like a brick poohouse, and I doubt my chances," he says. "I hope my individuality comes into it. I almost put the windows through any place I sing in." Uh-oh. But when he faces the judges, there are no windows to break. Instead, nervous Rik launches into his rendition of "Try A Little Tenderness" and melts the judges' (usually icy) hearts. They are impressed.

"You've got a great voice, a fantastic voice," says Pete. Rik goes through to the next auditions.

Rachel can't stop talking. She's sitting in the "holding area" waiting her turn. She's the last in her round, and she's feeling very nervous. Rumours by now are a-buzzing around the building – that the judges are cruel, the room is intimidating, and no one's getting through.

"If they're going to be critical," says Rachel, "then they should also help you."

Rachel drives a coach in Melton Mowbray, Leicestershire. She wants to be famous, she doesn't want to be a coach driver. She arrived with her trusty brolly, Frederick, and takes it in to the audition. This tickles the judges, as does her roaring rendition of "Downtown" (ancient tune by Petula Clark). Rachel goes through. Phew.

Behind the scenes

Do these judges know their onions, or are they mere part-timers in it for the TV cameras? Well, we can exclusively reveal that the four pros talk about nothing but pop – and Pete Waterman never shuts up!

PETE'S FAVOURITE TOPICS:

1. His experience of 1960s Northern Soul nightclubs.

2. The Ferrari restaurant in Milan he took Westlife to.

3. His years as a top record producer (which usually include the line "I wouldn't ever slag any of my artists off, life's too short").

4. Resurrecting the pop career of Ant and Dec. "He keeps on at us, but we say no," says a startled Ant.

5. And, er, the bath next to his bed. ("That's very important to me, having a bath next to my bed.")

Pete is a loving, generous man – he is always sharing his experiences with everyone.

The four are avid pop fans and take their jobs on *Pop Idol* very seriously. They debate for hours the whys and wherefores of finding a Pop Idol and they argue amongst themselves over little things – but are all agreed that their search is for someone with that X-factor. There's no other way of describing it. Well, they say that, anyway.

MOST POPULAR SONGS

The judges have been hearing many people... singing the same songs. Pete's thinking of banning the most popular, which are:

Anything by WESTLIFE

RONAN'S "When You Say Nothing At All"

TOM JONES'S "Sex Bomb"

CHRISTINA AGUILERA'S "Genie In A Bottle"

Anything by ANASTACIA

THE BANGLES' "Eternal Flame"

ROBBIE WILLIAMS' "Eternity"

Anything by SHAGGY

"Teletubbies" and "Bob The Builder"

Through to London

LAST NIGHT

Last night there was a delightful finger buffet at the hopefuls' hotel, where the judges gave a studied overview of the industry and what this *Pop Idol* prize would actually involve.

"We went through the legal side, the implications," says Nice Nicki. **"The serious side of it. A lot of people go to auditions and don't realise what they're doing."**

Simon was booed when he walked in the room. Oh dear. Fair Foxy was surprised at some of the questions from the floor.

"People were asking about how strict the management company was going to be," he says. "They're very wary, they've read too much stuff in papers. The last people they should be wary of are us! If someone's giving you a chance to play for Man United, you don't worry about wearing a red shirt."

Pernickity Pete, again, was blunt. Kelly asked him whether she would be able to have some input in the songwriting. Blam! Pete went ballistic.

"Do you want to be a pop star or do you want to be a writer?" he snorted. **"You can't do both. You come here, someone offers to give you two million pounds and the first question you ask is, 'Can I write the songs?' No! You ain't even got that far yet!"**

Now Pete is booed. If the talk could have been an example of what our Pop Idol might come up against, it worked very well – things are going to be tough. Kelly, however, wasn't amused by Pete's "reality sandwich". She showed us her bullet belt and said, "This one's for Pete Waterman." Crikey. But she's not the only one.

TODAY

Back at the Criterion, where the auditions to find the final 50 are taking place, the judges are ready and this time they look more intimidating. They are lit harshly in the middle rows of the theatre, behind a makeshift table resting on the seats in front. The sheer gaping emptiness of the theatre makes the challenge harder. This is the real test. This could be Wembley. But ever-optimistic Foxy thinks it's a bonus.

"When you've got everyone on stage together," says Foxy, "it makes it easier to see the really good people. And in many ways singing on stage is more natural for them."

The auditionees take the stage in sevens, and one sings his or her chosen song to the darkened auditorium, then the next, then the next. Everyone looks terrified. Rachel, with the frog umbrella, is juggling to steady her nerves. The judges say nothing – no comment, no jokes, just a "Next!" from Simon. Ooh, Simon, you are awful!

Some of the hopefuls here today aren't quite on form.

"We've seen some really good people," says Nicki, ever the diplomat, but she adds, "We've also seen some people who got through the net."

"We all looked at each other," quoth Foxy, "and said, 'God, we must have been feeling really good that day.'"

24 people are to be chopped from the 100. Dec says, "It's horrible, I feel physically sick for them. It's like facing a firing squad." The panel have the bullets.

Kelly may have her own ammunition on her belt, but she has not gone through. Dec comforts her. "I just wanted another chance!" she sniffs. Aw. Dec comforts the unfortunate and hands out the "Turn it into a positive experience" and "We all make mistakes" like a true Agony Uncle, but many people are steely.

"There are fewer tears here than I've seen for Wonkey Donkey," says Ant, ruefully.

Simon leaves his hallowed desk and has a look upstairs.

"Every one of those people we rejected," he says, "every one of them knew they'd blown it. I think, with the winners, they have a different confidence."

Now the 76 remaining singers have to team up in threes. The girls will sing Aretha's "Say A Little Prayer", the boys The Drifters' "Up On The Roof". You can't move for cavorting trios on the stairs, in the lavs, in the bar. Gareth Gates can be spotted asking Darius for tips! Good Lord.

Many groups work reasonably well – a bit of formation dancing, a bit of harmony – and some work fantastically together, but some people just can't work in a group... Tut tut.

Callandria complains that Vanessa is bossing her about. "She just wound me up," she says, "I let it get to me, though I shouldn't have done. This isn't *Pop Group*, it's *Pop Idol*."

What the judges are judging...
Do we know yet?

By now, all the judges know everyone by name, although all the hopefuls have their *Pop Idol* number for reference. Ah, nice judges. A lot of the stickers are peeling off as they get mankier, but there's a fresh batch to get from the production office. No one can ever be without their *Pop Idol* sticker. It's the law.

As each of the seven leave the stage, the judges comment, off camera. Pete, obviously, is the loudest. "He's trouble, I tell you! He's grief!" "This is a joke! This is crazy!" says Pete, who, as we all know, cannot shut up.

Backstage, after they've all had their turn, the auditionees are terrified. Many are upset that the judges watched their performance for a few seconds, then spent the rest of the time with their heads bowed over the desk. "She didn't even look at me!" is the cry.

The judges do sit with a piece of paper in front of them, listing the performers, and mark them with a tick or a cross, according to Nicki.

"They think we're making a judgement straight away, but we're not," she says. "We're making a note of their hair and clothes so we can remember them and what they're singing."

Ah, nice Nicki. Still difficult to tell what they're looking for, though, isn't it?

Ant McPartlin has just spoken to the auditionees.

"They're sh***ing themselves," he says, politely. He and Dec are looking nervous for everyone. Don't they get caught up in it all!

Tomorrow we'll get to the last 50. And from then on, it's your vote that counts. Exciting, isn't it?

Boys' choice

TOM JONES'S "Sex Bomb"

ROBBIE WILLIAMS' "Rock DJ"

GEORGE MICHAEL'S "Fast Love"

Girls' choice

MADONNA'S "Like A Virgin"

SHANIA TWAIN'S "That Don't Impress Me Much"

KYLIE'S "Spinning Around"

Day two

It gets harder. Everyone has three songs to choose from. "This is the bit I hate," says Nicki, of the elimination process; she's feeling the strain and dislikes having to be so brutal. In fact, all the judges (even Pete!) have really taken the competition to heart. They're living it, man.

"Of course you get sentimental," says Nicki. "Certain characters I have liked and today we've had to be brutal with them. It's not very nice when you like somebody, they've got their confidence built and suddenly they've got a 'Sorry, no.'" **"I wish I could say I haven't been going to sleep, dreaming about all this," says Mr Waterman, "but it's taken over my life."**

Last night, Darius, Rachel and friends went on a midnight trip to Tower Records to get the CDs of the above songs because they didn't know them already. Some people have had just a couple of hours' sleep, as they've been practising all night.

Darius feels he hasn't "been able to give my all". Gareth does the obligatory wistful singalong to "Rock DJ". Haifa, curls abounding, thinks her version was "too over the top". No one thinks they've done themselves justice.

After the excitement of the performances, where everyone seemed to be shaking more after they went on than before, **it's the waiting. And waiting. And waiting.**

Hours go by as the judges battle it out as to who gets into the final 50. Everyone is exhausted but wired. They sit on the stairs and contemplate. Young Danny from Manchester, who has been nicknamed Chuffin' 'Ell by Ant and Dec (Dan's most-used expression), cannot move for stress. He lies down, backflips now forgotten, looking wan.

No one knows when the judges will be finished. We later learn that there have been some real battles – whether or not to keep Rik and Oliver being two of them. Sandwiches and slices of quiche remain uneaten in the upstairs bar area, and the atmos – ooh, you could cut it with a knife. It's down to our friend Darius to start the singalong, and engage Gareth in a bit of strumming as well. Extreme's "More Than Words" serves to strengthen the hopefuls' faith, and gets most of them singing. Shame the judges can't hear the trilling melodies now…

In groups, the would-be Pop Idols are called to the stage and told whether they are going through or not. Only one group won't get in, and no one knows which it will be, but they're all – awww – supportive of each other. Such camaraderie – will we see it later on when the going gets tougher? Will the tough get mean?

As the disappointed 11 go to ring their families to let them know they're not through, the lucky ones group on the stage and are congratulated by the judges.

"I know I've got my Pop Idol in front of me," says Nicki. And the place roars with a cheer that could startle a hibernating creature. A very sleepy one.

Heat one

3076 **ANDY LOVE**, 22

From: Berkhamsted, Herts

Sings: "Man In The Mirror", Michael Jackson

433 **ERROL EDWARDS**, 23

From: Basford, Nottingham

Sings: "Another Day In Paradise", Phil Collins

1315 **LEVERNE SCOTT ROBERTS**, 19

From: Winsford, Cheshire

Sings: "Can't Fight The Moonlight", LeAnn Rimes

3528 **JAYNE STALA**, 20

From: Lambley, Nottingham

Sings: "Isn't She Lovely", Stevie Wonder

2662 **HAIFA KAYALI**, 21

From: Chigwell, Essex

Sings: "Unbreak My Heart", Toni Braxton

2021 **PAULA-JADE CREMIN**, 16

From: Cricklewood, London

Sings: "The Greatest Love Of All", Whitney Houston

123 **ZOE BIRKETT**, 16

From: Darlington, County Durham

Sings: "One Moment In Time", Whitney Houston

722 **JULIANNA HOY**, 24

From: Warrington, Cheshire

Sings: "One For Sorrow", Steps

964 **CHRISTOPHER TAME**, 18

From: Thirsk, Yorkshire

Sings: "All Or Nothing", O-Town

1175 **GARETH GATES**, 17

From: Bradford, Yorkshire

Sings: "Flying Without Wings", Westlife

This is the first week of five, where the final fearsome fifty are whittled down to the trembling ten. We're at the Teddington studios on a sunny Monday, and everyone is engaging in a bit of vocal warm-up with David and Carrie Grant, singing teachers to the stars.

David and Carrie take our first ten through a blistering journey of top notes and tongue twisters. They have created a special song that involves a complicated tune sung at breakneck pace. "Who Is A Pop Idol? Me!" seems to confuse even the steeliest of songsters. This warms everyone's voices up, and then the real work begins.

Each of our ten have to pick a song and work on it over the next two days, in order to sing it to the judges at the end of Wednesday. Some people are having a little difficulty choosing a song. Paula-Jade is advised not to sing a Diana Ross song which features the line "Every time you touch me, I become a hero" because Paula is a teeny tiny 16, and not a 90-plus Diana Ross. Just kidding. Diana Ross is much younger. 21, surely. So Paula, as wee as she is, decides to show off her enormous tonsils with Whitney's "The Greatest Love Of All", which is enough to shatter most windows from here to… way over there.

Kate Thornton is here, presenting the live coverage for ITV2. She goes through the many emails that have

IDOL GOSSIP

Jayne's boyfriend filled her application form in, because *Jayne* isn't as confident about herself as he is!

Zoe's feet smelt out the green room for the whole three days she was in there.

Gareth was told not to speak by the voice coaches, who were worried he'd strain his singing voice, but he cheated.

Haifa was sent a bunch of posh flowers from a mysterious admirer called Dennis. She didn't know who he was.

Paula-Jade claims she has chips with almost every meal.

Julianna brought the same top with her as *Leverne*, but lovely *Leverne* chose something else to wear.

Errol got emails proposing marriage from a legion of fans.

Andy now regrets stuffing a toy tiger down his trousers to sing "Rock DJ". He's had no end of grief from his mates.

inundated the programme since it began. Most are from admirers, some from friends.

While sitting in the green room, some contestants go through their songs, singing them quietly in the corner, while others read magazines and try to spot the Pop Idol coverage. There's a lot of it, even at this stage, with Gareth definitely a press favourite. But gadzooks! If you'd imagined an atmosphere of tense rivalry you'd be completely wrong. Everyone is – disappointingly – supportive.

Each Pop Idol contestant trots off to work with Carrie, and she goes through each song with a fine-tooth comb. She has a technique: to enable the sentiment of the song to come through, she asks questions all the way through as the singer sings. For example, as Gareth sings "Flying Without Wings":

Gareth: "You find it in the strangest places… "

Carrie: "Can you give me some suggestions, Gareth, as to where I might find it?"

Gareth: "Some find it in the face of their children…"

Carrie: "And then what do we think?"

Gareth: "Who can deny the joy it brings… "

Carrie: "And what's it like?"

Gareth: "You're flying without wiiiiings…"

And so on. It makes each song sound like a bizarre comedy sketch. But it works, it really does, and adds more weight to every performance. Makes it a lot more professional. After three days, it's time to show the audience at home, and the pesky judges, what they're made of. Cowell, Waterman, Chapman and Fox come along to give their input… but it's not as easy a ride as some thought it would be. Lulled by a comfortable atmosphere and the astonishing good feeling among contestants, it's a shock to hear the honest views of the judges – even Ant and Dec are cringing. So when Simon Cowell utters his steely comments – "It looked like you thought you didn't stand a cat in hell's chance of winning the competition" and "I ask, 'Has this person got what it takes to be number-one star in the country?' I say, 'No'" – the good atmosphere melts. Jayne, Paula-Jade and Julianna are upset because

Simon has laid into them. On the other hand, Errol is taken aback because Simon likes him. These judges! What are they like? Awful! But not to worry, they don't vote, you do.

But still… Simon. Pih!

The votes are in. Gulp.

The top five in reverse order are, with percentage of votes:

5th 6% Julianna Hoy

4th 7% Chris Tame

3rd 9% Haifa Kayali

2nd 10% Zoe Birkett

1st 62% Gareth Gates

There's been an excruciating 1.3 million voters deciding the fate of our cuddly tensome. Leverne wants to do it all again, Haifa feels like jelly, all Zoe says is she tried her best. All are crumbling with anticipation.

It turns out that up till the last few minutes, Zoe and Haifa were at level pegging.

Must have been the shiny trousers, Gareth. Time to wander back to the hotel, for eight to drown their sorrows and two to celebrate.

Heat two

121 **JOANNE BIRCHALL**, 24

From: Walton, Liverpool

Sings: "Chain Reaction", Steps/Diana Ross

753 **HAYLEY EVETTS**, 25

From: Quinton, Birmingham

Sings: "I Have Nothing", Whitney Houston

4649 **NIKK MAGER**, 17

From: Halifax, Yorkshire

Sings: "When You Say Nothing At All", Ronan Keating

3708 **DAVID WILSON**, 25

From: Gateshead, Tyne and Wear

Sings: "Love Is All Around", Wet Wet Wet

3828 **JONATHAN CAMPBELL**, 18

From: Glasgow, Scotland

Sings: "Deeper Shade Of Blue", Steps

3972 **LAURA DOHERTY**, 19

From: Derry, Northern Ireland

Sings: "Tears In Heaven", Eric Clapton

5723 **CHRIS GAZZARD**, 22

From: Bromley, Kent

Sings: "Lately", Stevie Wonder

6150 **KATIE NEIMAN**, 17

From: Hove, Sussex

Sings: "From This Moment", Shania Twain

6256 **KERRY PITT**, 23

From: Hemel Hempstead, Herts

Sings: "Touch Me In The Morning", Diana Ross

6524 **NICOLA THOMAS**, 22

From: East Finchley, London

Sings: "Finally", Ce Ce Peniston

Tuesday morning and again the studio at Teddington Lock buzzes with song. Carrie is asking her usual questions as she goes through everyone's song and David's telling everyone not to hold the microphone up to their nose, as you can't see anything but forehead. Others are told to give a "camera-sized" performance, as a stagier "Look At My Arms Wiggling" rendition looks like over-acting to the viewers. "Uncle" Mike Dixon accompanies everyone on piano, and he gives advice too. He thinks this lot is different from last week.

"When they first came in," he says, standing by his trusty piano, "there wasn't an initial feeling of the potential of these people. But they've grabbed hold of the gauntlet and become gladiators. They've come on leaps and bounds, even Jonathan."

Wee Jonathan, a little scamp from Glasgow with spiky hair, is finding it tough, says Uncle M. "I feel that Jonathan has slipped through the net. He's a nice lad, but they shouldn't put him through this. He should stick to singing in his choirs."

Around the green room, there's more entertainment laid on this week (there's a lot of time spent sitting, waiting to sing), with Connect Four and some board games. In the corner of the studio is the latest and most popular addition – a punch bag with Simon Cowell's face on it.

David, the Robbie Williams lookalike, was in the last 30 for *Popstars*, but says this competition is completely different. "*Popstars* was a bit more intense," he says. "There was a large volume of people in one room, you were

Idol Gossip

Chris once auditioned for Steps and very nearly got in, but thinks because H was already in the band they didn't feel they could take two blond men!

Hayley, once seen on Popstars, is Nicky's inspiration. "I saw you on TV and you really got me into singing and trying to make it!" gushes Nicky.

Joanne was given a lucky ring by her niece with an L on it for luck... but the L fell off.

David likes playing practical jokes – putting cellophane over toilet seats is his speciality.

"I had NOTHING bad to say about them!" he booms. "They were all indifferent." Oh. Simon reveals he has had a few hate emails thus far. "I'll print them off for you if you like." Well, we won't spend all our life waiting for that one, will we?

When the votes come in, everyone looks steely. Then Laura and her mum find out there's a story on the website about her they don't like, and tempers flare. Laura doesn't want to be broadcast on the 10pm results final if the story isn't taken off immediately… which duly happens. Nerves, eh? Finally, when everyone's calmed down, the results are broadcast:

Results:

5th 7.6% Nicky Thomas

4th 8.3% Katie Neiman

3rd 11.5% David Wilson

2nd 30.8% Laura Doherty

1st 33.2% Hayley Evetts

"I feel I've changed so much this week," admits Hayley, still beaming. "The voice coaches have transformed me. I really am that rough diamond who has been polished up."

While the *Pop Idollers* and assorted parents sob with emotion, Ant and Dec are happy to hug Hayley in her tight-fitting suit (stuck on with toupe tape). David reveals he's just found out his grandad died on Thursday, and it's been a very difficult day. Nicki takes it upon herself to tell him that although he didn't go through, someone will spot him because he has that X-factor. Oh yes.

brought out of the room, walked the walk, told what you were like, and it was pretty brutal. There's a relaxed atmosphere here. I'm not so nervous."

When the hopefuls come to perform their songs, the easy-going atmosphere changes and turns tense. The nerves are all too apparent – and it's not long before bubbly Nicky, the last of the ten to perform, stops bubbling and starts blubbing. She can't be stopped, and she hasn't even been on yet.

Ant and Dec have to do their old Agony Aunt routine. Had they expected this?

"I had a feeling we might have to put our arms round some shoulders," says Ant, "but I didn't think we would get so many tears. I've been taking tips from the end of *Family Fortunes* where Les Dennis comforts the woman who hasn't won the car."

"Unfortunately we can't shake off these pesky judges," says Dec. "I thought once we got out of the audition process then that would be the end of it, plain sailing. But they are very harsh. I don't think Simon's the most tactful person in the world."

"The judges don't sit with the contestants like we do," says Ant, mournfully. "They don't see how nervous they are. One criticism completely throws them."

And how. Hayley is told she is the best thing since sliced bread and beams like a woman possessed. But Chris and Jonathan are mauled by Simon, who doesn't think they were good enough – oh, let's not even quote him this week, he said the usual nasty stuff. Nicki tells him off at least twice. Most are surprised at Pete's turn-around. He refuses to say anything bad about Katie's performance because she has to go back to school the next day – was this because poor 16-year-old Paula-Jade was savaged the week before? Pete is none too forthcoming when asked.

Heat three

7 ANDREW DERBYSHIRE, 19

From: Burnley, Lancashire

Sings: "Wind Beneath My Wings", Bette Midler

95 ANTHONY BATEY, 17

From: Rugeley, Staffordshire

Sings: "Against All Odds", Phil Collins

988 CHRISTOPHER MASON, 21

From: Solihull, West Midlands

Sings: "Don't Let The Sun Go Down...", Elton John

2514 JESSICA GARLICK, 20

From: Kidwelly, South Wales

Sings: "Crazy For You", Madonna

3260 ROSEMARY RIBBONS, 18

From: Alltwen, South Wales

Sings: "Everything I Do", Bryan Adams

4055 SANDI MCCASH, 16

From: Dundee, Scotland

Sings: "Perfect", Eddie Reader

2907 OLIVER MANSON, 16

From: Stanmore, Middlesex

Sings: "I Swear", All-4-One

5483 HELEN FARRAR, 20

From: Luton, Bedfordshire.

Sings: "Say A Little Prayer", Aretha Franklin

5865 SURAYA KLEIN-SMITH, 23

From: Bethnal Green, London

Sings: "Don't Want To Miss A Thing", Aerosmith

6665 CARLA WINTERS, 22

From: Croydon, Surrey

Sings: "Get Here", Oleta Adams

Kate Thornton is following each and every one of the 50 for ITV2. "I'd worry for anybody who's about to step into this," she says, on the rigours of fame. "I don't think it's ever been as hard as it is now to be a public person. The media is bigger and more widespread than before. I don't know how I'd cope with the attention they're going to get. I would hate that."

And this week we see what the media can do. The gossip is that Rik Waller's fiancée has gone to the newspapers claiming Rik and Carla Winters are having an affair and that she and Rik split because of Carla. Carla's here, and she seems fit to face any questioning. In fact, she seems to relish the attention.

Rik and she are, she says, just good friends. They've been chatting since the Criterion auditions, sending each other text messages and singing together as part of Carla's band Tramp. She says Rik was about to split with his fiancée anyway, and that she stops him from going to auditions. She shows *The Official Pop Idol Book* a text message Rik sent early this morning, which *The Book* is shocked to see is a bit... saucy. "Ooh," she says. "He's just having a laugh. He has a heart of gold." Carla, however, says she fancies Simon Cowell. Good Lord.

Jessica sits on the green-room sofa and when the subject of Pete Waterman comes up, she doesn't shut up for hours. And hours and hours. You may remember, she

Idol Gossip

Anthony pays £10 to have his eyebrows plucked – although some of the press reporters on Tuesday thought this made him look a bit American Psycho. Gulp.

Andrew, like Britney, is a Pop Virgin. He says, "I haven't got the time for romance. I want to concentrate on my career." Crikey.

Sandi's so wee she has some of her clothes made for her. "Nothing ever fits," she shrieks, a mere two foot three (well, nearly).

Suraya's been matchmaking some of the gay Pop Idol contestants – with, she claims, great success. Her mobile ring tone is Destiny's Child's "Bootylicious".

Ollie has a banana phobia and won't go near them.

Jessica says that she thinks her idol Pete Waterman is divorced, and if they got together she might be Number One "in a week".

At first, we reckon Simon's calmed down this week, but then he lays into Ollie, then it's Foxy who fights back!

"This guy," says Fox on Oliver, "he's not a murderer, he's come here to sing… You're in danger of becoming a caricature, a pantomime dame."

Simon looks genuinely shocked. "I do not want to hurt his feelings intentionally," he says, "but this is what the music industry is like."

Anthony doesn't fare well with Pete, who says it's the worst performance of the series so far. Anthony doesn't care, although his eyebrows flap about a bit 'cos he knows it's up to the public vote. Oh, it is. Rosie, who originally made Pete cry, ends the show on a tonsil-tingling note. "This girl's a superstar," says Pete. And Simon agrees. The world, yes, has gone mad.

Results:

5th 8.3% Christopher Mason

4th 8.5% Sandi McCash

3rd 8.8% Ollie Manson

2nd 12.4% Jessica Garlick

1st 51.2% Rosie Ribbons

Doing it for Wales, Rosie and Jessica are ecstatic. Jessica's extra pleased, of course, because she gets to meet Pete again…

kissed Pete at her first audition, and he loved it. But poor man, does he know what he's in for this week? The edited highlights of her monologue go something like this:

"It was fantastic to be in his company… He was so lovely to me… I hope I'll be able to cope seeing him again… Be cool! Be calm!.. He's so high up in the industry! Ooooooh!" Etc. Jessica's got it bad. Chuffin' 'Ell.

Not so excited is Helen, who's spooked. She's been chatting with David Singing Teacher and he's guessed lots of things about her that she would hardly tell anyone. "Perhaps he's just very perceptive," someone pipes up. "Hmm…" says Helen. Later, after she's practised her song with Carrie, she marches evilly towards the Simon Cowell punch bag and rips into it – eyes firey with passion.

Sandi rushes off to the toilets all the time because she's so nervous. Meanwhile, Carla has got another text from Rik. It's 12.20pm and he hasn't got up yet. Ms Winters looks quite touched by this morning's series of communications. It all seems a bit odd to us, but we'll have to find out what happens as the weeks progress, won't we? Meanwhile, there's the small problem of getting the songs sorted out for Saturday's show… Come on now everybody, concentrate…

On the night, nerves abound. Sandi runs off in tears again when it comes to her turn, and has to be dragged back.

Pop Idol Extra

Rik's dad has been ringing up complaining about the web coverage and a piece entitled "Dump The Fat One". However, the piece went on to say how silly Simon is and how Rik's chances are high.

Rumour was, Helen and Andrew were getting rather close… Will there be a Pop Idol wedding, our Cilla?

29 **NATALIE ANDERSON**, 20
From: Bradford, Yorkshire
Sings: "Hero", Mariah Carey

5627 **CALLANDRIA JONES**, 18
From: Lancaster, lives London
Sings: "Think Twice", Celine Dion

5443 **TANIA ELISE FOSTER**, 17
From: London
Sings: "Killing Me Softly", Dionne Warwick, Fugees

6182 **LUCINDA O'CONNELL**, 21
From: Nottingham, lives Enfield
Sings: "How Do I Live", LeAnn Rimes

6531 **CRAIG THOMAS**, 18
From: Cardiff, lives London
Sings: "I Believe I Can Fly", R Kelly

544 **SALLY GOODISON**, 22
From: Barnsley, Yorkshire
Sings: "Sisters Are Doin' It", Aretha Franklin and
Annie Lennox

554 **REBECCA GOVAN**, 23
From: Westhoughton, Manchester
Sings: "Out Of Reach", Gabrielle

6160 **KORBEN**, 21
From: Bedford, Herts
Sings: "From The Heart", Another Level

6389 **SCOTT SADARI**, 19
From: Nottingham, lives London
Sings: "You Got A Friend", James Taylor

6691 **WILLIAM YOUNG**, 22
From: Hungerford, Berkshire
Sings: "Light My Fire", The Doors

Just as Jessica Garlick loves Pete Waterman, Simon Cowell loves high-waisted trousers and Pete loves Ferraris, Sally loves eggs. There's a nutter in every group, and Sally can nut for England. She infamously told *Pop Idol* she wanted to be famous to buy a house, a garden and chickens… so she could have lots of eggs.

"I love eggs – boiled, scrambled, fried, fertilised" Whhhat? Her boyfriend works on a farm and she can get fresh eggs. But there are none in the green room – just a big bowl of sweets and some *Pop Idollers* warbling in the corner.

Carrie: "What do you believe?"

Craig: "I believe I can flyyyy…"

Carrie: "What else do you believe?"

Craig: "I believe I can touch the skyyyy…"

Carrie: "How often do you think about it?"

Craig: "Think about it every night and dayyyy…"

This week is a lot more chilled. In fact, everyone looks half asleep by Tuesday, when most of them have worked on their songs and are waiting to sing them to the assembled press, who will interview them afterwards. (Lucky for Sally, there's egg and cress sandwiches for lunch.)

Idol Gossip

Tania's favourite meal is Weetabix, butter and Bovril. Yuk!

Scott is a friend of hippy crooner Joni Mitchell, and has visited her in Beverly Hills.

Rebecca, on the reserve list, was going to ring the Pop Idol team to say she didn't want to be on the list so she could attend other auditions… but they rang her first and told her she was in, replacing Layla – who's only 15 and had told a little white lie on her application form.

Korben's real name is Chris Nibblett. He once had to take Anthea Turner to hospital because she jogged into his dad's car and hurt her eyebrow. True.

Craig has sung for the Queen, and met her, at the opening of the National Welsh Assembly.

Callandria is in a Hear'say tribute band, as Kym.

William won a competition to be in a boy band set by TV show This Morning… but "it didn't happen".

Because the series is in full swing and everyone's had a chance to watch it on the telly, no one is worried about the judges. With Ollie's triumph last week – a slating by the judges but No. 3 in the voting – hopes are high. The Public will decide, so sod Simon Cowell.

Tania, who admits she fancied Darius when she met him (but doesn't now, er, 'cos she's just got a boyfriend), sees it all as experience. "I'm only 17, so if the judges don't like me now, well… I've got a few years to get it right."

Callandria and Korben are arguing about the cameras.

"I love the camera," says Korben. "I prefer to perform to a glass screen than a person."

"I disagree," says Callandria. "I've never performed in front of a camera before, not even at an audition. It's something I have to get used to."

Korben, Callandria and Scott have all been going out with Suraya, Andrew and Anthony from last week, tripping the light fantastic. They're a talkative lot. Callandria recalls that Simon called her "very, very average" at her first audition and that she went over to the punch bag first thing and whopped him one. The punch bag has, not surprisingly, been receiving many blows – including one from a member of Westlife, who was at the studios at the end of last week and had to have a go (Simon is, of course, Westlife's A&R man).

Rehearsals continue, and it's clear that this lot are still finding their feet. Many miss their cues and need a bit of

help from Uncle Mike in finding their starting note. Hey, guys, it's not as easy as it looks. After they have all sung, Carrie and David give them detailed notes and then leave, to much consternation from the hopefuls. Now they're on their own, to face the TV cameras… and the judges.

And what an ordeal it turns out to be. Simon has not heeded Foxy's words last week and lays into Scott, who he describes as "flat and tuneless". Pete says Scott's is the worst vocal he's ever heard in his life. Tactful. Scott looks devastated, and Lucinda rushes on to the stage to give him a hug. Emotions are running high and no one wants to go on after such a slating. Korben is told he is cocky, and William's feisty performance doesn't wash with sly old Simon, who isn't impressed. Is the man crazy? Well, yes, he certainly could be.

And suddenly, Wishy-Washy Will (he keeps himself to himself, writing his diary away from the green room) turns into Warlord Will as he gives Simon a real ticking off – stopping Simon from interrupting him mid-flow – and speaks for every one of the ten. Oh, he does.

And it pays off!

Results:

5th 3.9% Rebecca Govan

4th 5.9% Tania Elise Foster

3rd 12.6% Natalie Anderson

2nd 24.7% Korben

1st 41.5% William Young

So this week, it's the boys who go through to the final ten. Weeping aside, after all the excitement, Will is steely about his win – only yesterday was he at the funeral of a family friend. Korben is extremely chirpy. "It's lovely to feel wanted," he says. Aw. Now that's not very cocky, eh, Simon?

80 HAYLEY BAMFORD, 20

From: Northshore, Blackpool

Sings: "Saving All My Love", Whitney Houston

97 AARON BAYLEY, 26

From: Walkerdene, Newcastle

Sings: "Walking In Memphis", Mark Cohn

5206 JADE CANNELL, 19

From: Waterlooville, Portsmouth

Sings: "Where Do Broken Hearts Go", Whitney Houston

1505 SARAH WHATMORE, 20

From: Worsley, Manchester

Sings: "Endless Love", Diana Ross and Lionel Richie

2545 RIK WALLER, 20

From: Rainham, Kent

Sings: "I Can't Make You Love Me", George Michael

3778 DARIUS DANESH, 21

From: Bearsden, Glasgow

Sings: "Something Inside So Strong", Labi Siffre

1349 JOANNE SLATTERY, 24

From: Marshside, Southport

Sings: "Relight My Fire", Take That

5223 VANESSA CAVANAGH, 18

From: Greenford, Middlesex

Sings: "End Of The Line", Honeyz

5996 RACHEL MAKINS, 21

From: Melton Mowbray, Leicestershire

Sings: "Torn", Natalie Imbruglia

6570 DAVINA PERERA, 24

From: Orpington, Kent

Sings: "Total Eclipse Of The Heart", Bonnie Tyler

Can you feel the love in the room?

The frank answer is no. This bunch, the very last week of the final 50, is – as Mr Rik Waller so quaintly puts it – the Group Of Death.

Alarmist, but it does help explain the nerves here at Teddington Studios. After weeks of Sly Simon letting rip at a bunch of extremely fearful singers people are so tense they bite their nails (Rik, especially), they cry (Rachel) or they… fall asleep (Davina).

Of course, no one will admit to being that pressurised, but on Tuesday David Grant has to have a word with everyone about their attitude. He thinks that many of the group are putting very little energy into their performance. This, he feels, is because some reckon that Rik and Darius – measuring the amount of column inches each has had since the contest began – are the sure-fire winners. Not so! says David. It doesn't work like that. He urges them to put more effort into their performance, to stop being "lacklustre", but it takes time for this to set in. Where are your guts, *Pop Idollers*? Stop moaning and get on with it.

Vanessa is in no mood for such comments. "I was gutted when he said that," she cries. "This is what I want to do and I'm putting everything into it. David was saying, 'Look like you want to be here, otherwise just go.' Some people say they're bored, but I've not been bored once."

Rik's not bored; he'd chat to a lamppost if he stood near it long enough. He's diplomatic on the Carla story, and

Idol Gossip

Aaron's girlfriend has a Posh fixation and says if he wins Pop Idol they're going to buy the gatehouse in the grounds of Posh's house, and apparently she's already got a sports car on order…

Hayley used to fancy Robbie when he was in Take That. Hayley's dad is a dead ringer for Simon Cowell! Hmm.

Rachel had bruises from Monday, when *Darius* span her chair round so hard she fell off.

Rik had a bad throat and spent his time drinking yukky linctus.

Darius has printed autograph cards to give his public. *Simon Cowell* rang him after the Criterion show was broadcast to apologise for calling him corny! The sly beggar.

Darius has grown up a bit – and he'd be the first to tell you that. Now he's shaved off his goatee and cut his hair he looks, well, less cult leader. Although the man might not want to say he can feel the love in the room (and there's not much about, anyway), he can still come out with that old spook stuff. Earlier he told Kate Thornton about his two brothers. "To meet them is intriguing, to know them is amazing, to love them is divine." Is he sending himself up here?

Hayley is not so away with the fairies. She says the judges don't bother her, but if they're rude she won't know what to say. "I'd like to say something like, 'Kiss my arse, Simon'… but I don't think I will." Go on! Do it!

David spends more time giving pep talks to some of the ten. He's telling them to go for it, to concentrate on their performance.

"I tell you," he says, "it's not about who goes through or not. There will be someone in the fifty who – in a couple of years – eclipses the winner. Don't think about Simon – he rejected Craig David and David Gray, two of the biggest solo singers in the last few years. Remember, this is your showcase." Hoorah.

says they're great friends and work professionally. He's cynical about his ex-girlfriend, who sold her story to not one but two newspapers – in an attempt to get him back, he says. However, the love wasn't there.

"I've probably been saved," he says, freed from the relationship of two and a half years. "Not from a life of misery as such… but when the bad times outweigh the good…" Uh-oh. He later claims she spent all his money too.

Darius could also chat to a lamppost if he stood near it – but he would stand very close indeed. He explains how he was "petrified" about doing the auditions, as he couldn't afford to fail twice.

"I rang up Nigel Lythgoe," he recalls. "He said, 'I don't even know if you'd get through the first round. We've got a bloke called Simon Cowell…' I thought it might ruin my chances of getting ahead in music again, until my brother said to me on the day of the auditions, 'If you apply for a job and don't get it, does that stop you applying for all jobs?' So I went to the auditions."

On the night, nerves abound. Simon has a go at fluey Rik, calling him conceited: "I think all this has gone to your head." From new TV chat-show guest Simon! Good gracious. Pete thinks Rik sounds like Harry Secombe. Rik wasn't happy but did not storm off set, as reported by the "gentlemen" of the press. Rachel is told she shouldn't have left her lucky frog umbrella behind, because she looks nervous, so Dec runs on to the stage to give it to her. But Simon's a different character when Sarah walks on. "I've only got two words for you," he says. "Marry me!" Eurgh!

Results:

5th Vanessa Cavanagh 3.5%

4th Sarah Whatmore 19.8%

3rd Darius Danesh 19.9%

2nd Aaron Bayley 24.9%

1st Rik Waller 25.6%

And so Rik and Aaron stroll away merrily into the night, pleased as punch that they got through. Aaron in particular is pleased, as he wasn't initially a press favourite. Must have been his bad dancing that melted the nation's heart.

Pop Idol Extra

Simon Cowell *was stunned when he discovered that his mother and brother had talked to the press about him and given them a stack of embarrassing photos, including one showing him wearing a bra and make-up!*

Simon *said: "When Mum told me she had shown a journalist some photos, my stomach felt like I was in a fast lift going down quickly. I knew immediately what picture they would use."*

Hayley Evetts

Any advice from mum and dad?
They just told me to enjoy it. "We want you to win, but if you don't we're still really proud of you," which is nice to know.

What was in your school report?
I really loved school, and they were always fine. I wasn't naughty or anything like that. I haven't looked at my reports for years – I left school ten years ago.

Qualifications
I think I got about seven or eight GCSEs but I was really ill when I was 14 and I had to have eight months off school. I went down to six and a half stone because I had TB. The school didn't send me any work. I had to drop maths and another language. I was upset 'cos I loved school!

Hobbies
I don't go to the gym religiously or anything. I'd say I just watch loads and loads of telly! *Friends* and *Buffy*.

Have you ever wanted to be a plumber?
I always wanted to be a nurse. I wanted to work in intensive care. I'd be a nurse if I wasn't doing this. Bit different, pop star and nurse, aren't they?

Favourite film
Grease.

Favourite record
"Under The Moon Of Love" by Showaddywaddy.

First popstar crush
Matt Goss from Bros. Whoa! I was at home when "Drop The Boy" came out, eating my tea, saw him on the telly and thought, He's lurvverly! It was the quiff.

Do you have a lucky gonk?
I've got a roomful. The main one is a book on Elvis that I was trying to get hold of for six years, which was discontinued. Someone bought it for me from America, so now I carry that round with me all the time. It's called

Elvis – What Happened – it's about his rise to fame and his fall.

Thing you can't live without
Hair straighteners. My hair's really curly. It's just frizz.

Worst hair day
Remember when Kylie was big first time round and she had that shaggy perm? My mum's hairdresser did this perm on me, and it was like candyfloss. It shrunk into tight little curls round my head. Urgh!

Person you'd like to be stuck in a lift with?
Dead or alive? Either? Elvis. I don't know what I'd say. I think he's gorgeous, but I think I'd be intimidated. I'd suppose I'd ask why he never came to England to tour.

Most-used expression
"Fantastic."

If you could be anyone for the day who would you be?
Kylie Minogue.

What will you buy with your first million?
A Z3 sports car.

Can you wire a plug???
Yes.

What's the weirdest thing that's been written about you?
That I was in Hear'say. They claimed I was the first member.

Your ambition in three words:
Successful, Loaded, Liked.

RIK Waller

Any advice from mum and dad?
It's the same as they always said – get plenty of rest and make sure you do your best. They always trust my judgement.

What was in your school report?
My best subjects were art and drama. All the other reports would say, "He's very lazy."

Qualifications
I don't see those as something important to me – in other words, I don't have any, ha! I left school when I was 15. I think the real qualifications in this life are those you get through experience.

Hobbies
Pool and snooker. I also love a game of football. It's one of those things that you wouldn't think I'd be any good at, but trust me, when I get my weight behind that ball it flies. And I've got a lot of weight to put behind it.

Have you ever wanted to be a plumber?
No, but I wouldn't mind being a basketball player.

Favourite film
Snatch by Guy Ritchie.

Favourite record
"Heaven" by Bryan Adams.

First popstar crush
Not anyone in particular. I always listened to music for music, not particularly the person behind it. I didn't look at it like that.

Do you have a lucky gonk?
I wear my nan's sovereign, which was put in a ring for my dad for his 50th birthday. It's St George and the dragon. It was passed on to my grandmother by her grandmother, then given to my dad because he always loved it. Now me.

Thing you can't live without
Chocolate. It's my weakness. Put me in front of a super-model or a bar of chocolate, I'd have trouble deciding which one to go for.

Worst hair day
I once had it almost down to my shoulders. The problem is my hair's very curly, so it looked like I had a perm, which was quite bad.

Person you'd like to be stuck in a lift with?
Someone intelligent, someone you could have a good chat with.

Most-used expression?
Couple of years ago it used to be "Oo-er". We're all saying Aaron's thing now – "Spot on!"

If you could be anyone for the day who would you be?
George Michael. I've admired him for years.

What will you buy with your first million?
I would set up a trust account for my nieces, and I'd also like a pair of Nike Air Jordans.

Can you wire a plug???
Yes.

What's the weirdest thing that's been written about you?
Me apparently telling *Pop Idol* they could "shove the show up their arse". I had no knowledge of that whatsoever.

Your ambition in three words:
Achieve Personal Best.

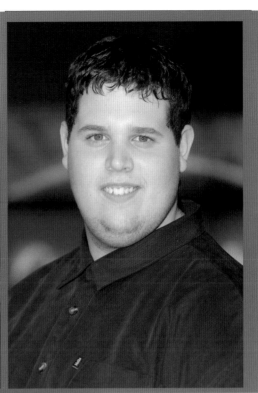

AARON Bayley

Any advice from mum and dad?
Just to be myself. They know that I'm taking it one day at a time.

What was in your school report?
I was a quiet, shy lad at school, and hard-working. It was only when I got the job at the Bingo and I was working with people all the time that I started to open up a bit more.

Qualifications
I passed all my GCSEs – I've got eight – and I've got a National Diploma in Music and Performing Arts. I play guitar – self-taught.

Hobbies
Computers and football – supporting Newcastle United. I build computers from separate components. I did two for my mate this Christmas and I saved him about £400 on each one.

Have you ever wanted to be a plumber?
I wanted to be a policeman when I was a kid, and still did up until the point I decided I wanted to sing instead.

Favourite film
Rain man with Dustin Hoffman.

Favourite record
REM's "Everybody Hurts", as well as Elvis's "Anything That's Part Of You". I don't know!

First popstar crush
Can you remember a band called Spagna, when that song was out, "Call Me"? I saw the video – and I had a bit of a crush on her.

Do you have a lucky gonk?
I suppose my lucky emblem is a Hard Rock Cafe guitar my mum and dad brought back from New York. Either that or my Hard Rock Cafe boxer shorts… Don't ask!

Thing you can't live without
My guitar. I've been playing "Babylon" by David Gray recently.

Worst hair day
I cut my hair myself, and one day I forgot to put the hair clipper guard on and I went up the side of it, and shaved it all off! I had to do the whole lot like that, and I looked like an idiot.

Person you'd like to be stuck in a lift with?
Apart from my girlfriend – someone classy, Jennifer Aniston.

Most-used expression
The one that's become a hit with all this lot is "Spot on!" Rik's nicked that off me.

If you could be anyone for the day who would you be?
Elvis Presley. The young Elvis, in '56, when he was about 18.

What will you buy with your first million?
My girlfriend would probably want a boob job. I'd want an executive suite at St James's Park and a Lamborghini Diablo.

Can you wire a plug???
Aye. That's a funny question, isn't it? I can build computers but I can't wire a plug?! Of course I can.

What's the weirdest thing that's been written about you?
I haven't had that much publicity, to be honest with you. People are only starting to get my name spelt right nowadays.

Your ambition in three words:
Stardom, Fame, Recognition.

JESSICA Garlick

Any advice from mum and dad?
My mum always tells me to pray, which I do anyway. Obviously to do my best – plenty of water, plenty of sleep.

What was in your school report?
Every one of them said I was confident – quite bossy, actually. They say "Jessica is a born leader." I couldn't concentrate in class because I always wanted to sing.

Qualifications
I've got GCSEs and I did a performing arts course for two years, a BTEC.

Hobbies
I'm a little homemaker, to be honest. I love baking cakes. I make fantastic little fairy cakes! They're so soft! I make shortbread. I love sewing, making clothes… [Intense beam in eye.] I love cleaning, I love things to be clean! [Gulp.]

Have you ever wanted to be a plumber?
I Never ever wanted to be anything but a singer. I did my first stage performance when I was three. I loved it – the applause! – I was addicted.

Favourite film
Coming to America with Eddie Murphy.

Favourite record
I've got a few. Aerosmith, "Don't Want To Miss A Thing". My favourite song to sing is "Like A Prayer" by Madonna.

First popstar crush
Robbie Williams when he was in Take That. Goodness me, I was really going to marry him, 100 per cent – there was no doubt in my mind, absolutely!

Do you have a lucky gonk?
No. The power of prayer is all I take, and my lozenges, but that's it.

Thing you can't live without
Water, I suppose. I drink about four litres a day. I wee all the time – every half an hour!

Worst hair day
When I was eight, all my friends had fringes so I decided to have one cut. I had this great whopping nasty fringe right over my eyebrows and it looked awful. I used to tie it back as best I could.

Person you'd like to be stuck in a lift with?
In all the world? Probably Madonna. She couldn't get away from talking to me then!

Most-used expression
"Do you know what I mean?"

If you could be anyone for the day who would you be?
The Queen, so I could see what it's like inside the palace. I'd love to look around, to know what's in her fridge, what kind of loo roll she uses.

What will you buy with your first million?
A Porsche or something like that. A car that's pretty cool.

Can you wire a plug???
Yeah, pretty good with electrics. My dad's an electrician.

What's the weirdest thing that's been written about you?
They made me out to be a flasher in one tabloid. They wrote, "She once flashed her boobs and bum to local punters" and it was all by accident.

Your ambition in three words:
To Be Famous.

ZOE Birkett

Any advice from mum and dad?
Yeah, they just keep me right. Their advice is to enjoy it. It's not about winning, it's participating. Go there, do your best. If something comes of it that's brilliant. If not, there's always something else.

What was in your school report?
The worst were probably science and maths – not my strong points at all. In reports they say, "Zoe excels at music and performing, Spanish and Art." I'm not too fussed about science, though – I never wanted to be an inventor.

Qualifications
I got ten GCSEs and I failed in IT.

Hobbies
I dance, I play a little piano and I like to shop for clothes.

Have you ever wanted to be a plumber?
No, never. I used to want to be a dancer. I used to dance more than sing.

Favourite film
Forrest Gump.

Favourite record
"Funky Town" by Lips Inc.

First popstar crush
Jason Donovan, probably… No! It was Mark Owen from Take That. I loved him! I loved his hair. I went to see them. They all came down on stage in a circle and he pointed and I thought he pointed at me! He never did, but I was, "Ooh! Mark!"

Do you have a lucky gonk?
It's in my purse! Angel of Prosperity – a stone with an angel engraved on it.

Thing you can't live without
Cheesecake – I have it at least three times a week. I like strawberry and cherry best. It's a bit of an addiction, so recently I've had to calm down on it. [Looks serious.]

Worst hair day
When I take my extensions out my hair goes like a big frizzball. My hair needs a rest every month. It can look good on some people, but on me…

Person you'd like to be stuck in a lift with?
Elton John. I think he's fantastic. I'd talk to him about… everything. He seems so down to earth.

Most-used expression
"Yes yes" and [adopts strange US accent] "Damn right".

If you could be anyone for the day who would you be?
Maybe someone in this group to see what their view on this whole thing is.

What will you buy with your first million?
The first thing I'd buy is a boxer dog. My mum's got this cat called Fifi, a white Persian, and she's beautiful – my mum's pride and joy. I've always wanted a boxer and I'm not allowed one.

Can you wire a plug???
No. Never tried!

What's the weirdest thing that's been written about you?
The worst thing was when I got through and someone wrote, "Zoe was gutted that Gareth won." They were making out as if I was a horrible person.

Your ambition in three words:
Win Pop Idol!

WILLIAM Young

Any advice from mum and dad?
They say, "If you want advice then we'll give it," but I haven't asked. I'm from an independent family.

What was in your school report?
The worst was, "My heart sank when I learnt that William was in my class." I wasn't well behaved at school, but I managed not to get caught!

Qualifications
I've got ten GCSEs, three A-Levels in politics, ancient history and English – two As and a B; and a 2-2 in politics from Exeter University.

Hobbies
Lots of them. I do a lot of drawing, photography, running – any sport, really. I like walking, reading… I write films as well.

Have you ever wanted to be a plumber?
I wouldn't mind being a plumber. It's quite a friendly job, and you never get a nasty plumber.

Favourite film
Room with a View – no! Not that. The other one… The butler and… Ooh, er… [takes ages to remember] *Remains of the Day*!

Favourite record
Joan Armatrading, "Love And Affection".

First popstar crush
Probably Kylie, when I was about… 1987, when she first came out.

Do you have a lucky gonk?
I've got lucky trousers. I've lots of lucky things around, stuff I've picked up – stones and shells, and people. I keep them in my room… [Looks impish.] Just joking! [Hm.]

Thing you can't live without
My Minidisc Walkman, which is awful because I can come across as really anti-social.

Worst hair day
It was when I went on *This Morning*. I did a boy-band competition and I won it. The following week we went on for a makeover and they made me look like a monkey – they brushed down my fringe. Urgh!

Person you'd like to be stuck in a lift with?
Beverley Knight. She's very sexy, very cool.

Most-used expression
"Why do I do this to myself?" I am quite useless at most things. I'm really scatty. I make life as difficult as possible for myself.

If you could be anyone for the day who would you be?
Er… [Thinks for five million hours.] I think I'd be my twin brother for the day. That would be interesting.

What will you buy with your first million?
I want to get a new Mini. I'm a Mini buff.

Can you wire a plug???
Yes, I can. My dad taught me.

What's the weirdest thing that's been written about you?
I don't read much of the press we've been getting. I haven't read anything about me.

Your ambition in three words:
To Remain Happy.

LAURA Doherty

Any advice from mum and dad?
My family's very musical so they help me on the songs and the way I should perform. My dad knows if I'm out of tune. He helps me with breathing and phrasing. My dad's the only one I listen to.

What was in your school report?
A teacher once said to my mummy, "Don't forget to bring me on Laura's *This Is Your Life*." I was eight years old at the time.

Qualifications
I've got nine GCSEs and two A-Levels.

Hobbies
Talking, buying clothes – I love my style.

Have you ever wanted to be a plumber?
No, no! Maybe a dance teacher, but not that much.

Favourite film
The Shawshank Redemption with Tim Robbins.

Favourite record
"Thriller" by Michael Jackson.

First popstar crush
E17, Tony Mortimer – I loved him. I covered my wall with posters of him. He was very quiet, as I remember, but I liked those big baggy jeans.

Do you have a lucky gonk?
I've got my boyfriend's ring. He has no choice in the matter! I took it off him to wear. I do it every time we're at the airport.

Thing you can't live without
My phone. I've got a Pay As You Go. Over the last four days I've spent £70. I have to keep buying the cards. I spent about £22 this morning.

Worst hair day
When I was about ten I had all my curls cut off and my mummy cried for days!

Person you'd like to be stuck in a lift with?
Michael Jackson. I love his music. I'd suggest we do a concert together.

Most-used expression
"I'm grand!" [Said in Irish accent so the "d" falls off.]

If you could be anyone for the day who would you be?
I might be Samantha Mumba, 'cos she's my age and I want to do all that she has done.

What will you buy with your first million?
Lots of designer clothes. Everything for sale that I can't get! Everything!

Can you wire a plug???
I can, actually.

What's the weirdest thing that's been written about you?
That I was an ambassador for my city, Londonderry. I can't believe it, all I'm doing is singing, which I love so much. The other thing is I look like Beyoncé from Destiny's Child.

Your ambition in three words:
To Be Happy.

KORBEN

Any advice from mum and dad?
I'm left to my own devices. I'm the only music person in my family. If they did start suggesting things, I'd say, "What do you know?" They do help picking my songs, though.

What was in your school report?
"Chris could do so well if he turned up." In music, dance and drama it was excellent – they said I had "star quality".

Qualifications
Nine GCSEs, all bad grades – I'm dyslexic.

Hobbies
Rollerbooting round the roads, to the shops… It's quicker than walking, it really is.

Have you ever wanted to be a plumber?
No, maybe a TV presenter. No disrespect to plumbers.

Favourite film
Coyote Ugly, and *Pretty Woman*. I like a lot of films… *Interview With A Vampire*.

Favourite record
Burt Bacharach's "You'll Never Get To Heaven (If You Break My Heart)".

First popstar crush
Morten Harket from A-Ha. The cheekbones! And I like Andrea Corr – she's very good-looking.

Do you have a lucky gonk?
A good friend gave me a box of novelty plasters which I'll put on my body before I perform.

Thing you can't live without
Friends and family. I do need people around me.

Worst hair day
When I was about five I had a blond bowl haircut. One day I grabbed the front of my fringe and snipped right across. It took ages to grow back. My mum wasn't happy. I was her blond blue-eyed boy.

Person you'd like to be stuck in a lift with?
George Michael. I respect him as a producer and artist. I'd ask him how he's dealt with his sexuality over the

years. I'd ask him what it was like hiding it for so long, who he told, who he didn't.

Most-used expression
"I'm so chuffed!"

If you could be anyone for the day who would you be?
David Attenborough. He goes to interesting places. I'm a sea person. I love the sea.

What will you buy with your first million?
I'd get out of debt!

Can you wire a plug???
Yes… Er, no. I don't think I can.

What's the weirdest thing that's been written about you?
That I was dyslexic, meaning I'm not now. That's just impossible.

Your ambition in three words:
Individuality, Originality, Lovability.

GARETH Gates

Any advice from mum and dad?
To get as much rest as possible, not to be up too late the night before, take vitamins, eat loads of fruit and salad.

What was in your school report?
I'm a real hard worker at school. Am I a swot? A few people say that… I'm not a swot 'cos I'm bright. I have to work hard at it. My best subject is music and I love art, English language and maths.

Qualifications
GCSEs. I got seven As and three Bs. Most people concentrate only on their studies but I've always had the music side of things *and* the school side.

Hobbies
After school I sing in choirs, or on my own – I have singing lessons. I play guitar, piano and drums as well. I love a game of tennis, I like football, the odd game of golf here and there – but only pitch and putt.

Have you ever wanted to be a plumber?
Never. I've always wanted to get into music. If it wasn't that it would've been football.

Favourite film
The Green Mile or *Gladiator*.

Favourite record
I love Westlife, but I don't have a favourite song. With me, it's hard to say because I like every style: jazz, funk, pop, opera – everything, even rap.

First popstar crush
Britney Spears.

Do you have a lucky gonk?
My phone! No, nothing.

Thing you can't live without
My family.

Worst hair day
Today, perhaps. No, but it's a bit long, though. Up till the age of 12 it was a bit bowl cut. People used to make a joke that I used to put a bowl on my head and cut round it. Then after that, I had "curtains" for ages. Everyone had it, but when I look back, it looks pathetic.

Person you'd like to be stuck in a lift with?
Rachel from S Club 7. I do like her, but she's got a boyfriend. But I wouldn't want to be in a broken lift at all, really.

Most-used expression
Because of my stammer, I always go "Er, er", so probably that! Huh!

If you could be anyone for the day who would you be?
Me! No… Shane from Westlife because he's one of my idols.

What will you buy with your first million?
Sort all my family out, then after that I would love to – and I'm not saying this to win people over, this is genuine – I'd love to help people. The hungry, the homeless and the hurting. For people who are really deprived, in Africa and other places, I'd provide houses, food, medicine, warmth.

Can you wire a plug???
Yeah. I learnt that in science.

What's the weirdest thing that's been written about you?
That I'd overcome my stammer. To work so hard on something, then to do well, then for people say it was an act! It's obviously something I've really suffered with all my life.

Your ambition in three words:
To Help Others.

ROSIE Ribbons

Any advice from mum and dad?

They told me what the judges told me – to pick the right songs and to watch what I say on camera. I talk before I think sometimes.

What was in your school report?

I was really good up until the fifth form – the most important year of school – then I lost complete interest in every subject except drama, and they all said, "She can try harder." My worst was maths. I didn't understand anything. I was pathetic.

Qualifications

The only GCSEs I passed were drama and English. I didn't prepare for the other subjects.

Hobbies

I love reading. I like horror stories, and I'm reading some Black Lace – they're quite nice too, you know. I love getting into an old book. You can use your imagination a lot more.

Have you ever wanted to be a plumber?

No! When I was young I thought I might like to be a policewoman, but from eight onwards I couldn't see myself do anything else but sing.

Favourite film

Top Gun and Dirty Dancing.

Favourite record

I like so many different styles, it's hard to say one style. I like garage, I like it all. I even like classical, opera and things like that, but I hate rock and heavy metal, it's awful.

First popstar crush

I never really had one. I was never into the boy bands – they don't appeal to me. I see a lot of artists and think, You're yummy, but I've never done the teenage thing and bought the posters.

Do you have a lucky gonk?

A little black cat, a silver horseshoe and a four-leaf clover.

Thing you can't live without

Hund, my dog. I've had him since I was seven. I can't go anywhere without him. I cuddle him at night.

Worst hair day

When I was little, this boy used to pick on me all the time – he used to put plasticine and chewing gum in my hair, and my mother had to cut big clumps out.

Person you'd like to be stuck in a lift with?

Mariah Carey. She could sing to me and keep me occupied.

Most-used expression

"Fab!"

If you could be anyone for the day who would you be?

I know Jessica said this, but I'd like to be the queen too. You wonder about the royal family, and what they get up to. That would be quite interesting.

What will you buy with your first million?

I'd buy my mother a holiday to Australia to see her relatives and my father a pink plane. He wants one, for some reason, and it has to be pink.

Can you wire a plug???

Yes.

What's the weirdest thing that's been written about you?

Nothing really. It gets me how they keep spelling my name wrong. It's been Gibbons, Robins, Ribbens…

Your ambition in three words:

Be Successful Singer.

DARIUS Danesh

Any advice from mum and dad?
To really enjoy what you're doing. That's been the most important thing. I'm not doing this to become well known. *Popstars* achieved that end. I didn't need to come back.

What was in your school report?
I worked hard, but I was told that I tried too hard. I analyse too much. Funnily enough, Nigel Lythgoe said that on *Popstars* – that I tried too hard.

Qualifications
Of my standard grades [Scottish equivalent of GCSEs], I got eight. I have six Highers [A-Levels].

Hobbies
Rugby, windsurfing and skiing. I love playing sport, but I can't watch football or play it.

Have you ever wanted to be a plumber?
My grandfather worked as an engineer, on the docks on the River Clyde, and I remember being fascinated by that as a kid, seeing real hard work. From then I thought that whatever I did in life, it should be something I enjoyed. Not that I wanted to do what my grandfather did. My love has always been performing.

Favourite film
Léon, with Natalie Portman. It's a wicked film; an interesting, blockbusting take on an emotional idea…

Favourite record
"More Than Words" by Extreme, a classic track. It's the song that inspired me to pick up the guitar.

First popstar crush
Kylie. I bought her first album when I was eight years old. She was the kind of girl you wanted to childmind you.

Do you have a lucky gonk?
One of my best friends gave me an ancient volcanic piece of rock. Apparently it brings good luck for singers. And I must be the luckiest, happiest boy in Britain.

Thing you can't live without
My family. I wouldn't be here without them.

Worst hair day
I think that's an easy question to answer. The ponytail! I looked like a cross between a slicked-back pimp and a dodgy Greek waiter…

Person you'd like to be stuck in a lift with?
Sean Connery. I completely rate him. I once met him at a film premiere and I asked him what advice he would give me. He said, "Darius, you've only ever failed when you stopped trying."

Most-used expression
"Wicked."

If you could be anyone for the day who would you be?
One of my family, to see what I'm like.

What will you buy with your first million?
I will invest. I would love to buy the dream home for my parents, but I don't want to buy anything for me.

Can you wire a plug???
Yes, course I can, I studied physics.

What's the weirdest thing that's been written about you?
"Darius pays to date girls." According to one newspaper I spent £500 a week to some dating service to be seen in public with different girls. I was seeing a girl at the time and it upset her, but she knew it was a ludicrous story.

Your ambition in three words:
Light, Life, Love.

Calling on the experts

DAVID AND CARRIE'S SINGING TIPS

1. Think about who you're singing to – are you on your own, are you talking to one other person or a whole group? This is what David and Carrie poshly call the three "circles of concentration".

2. "Throat lozenges are bad for you!" says Carrie. "They won't help your sore throat. Drinking water will."

3. Sing songs you can relate to. "Know the emotional journey of the song so you can connect with it," says David. "If you're 16, don't sing a song about divorce."

4. Sing it your way; find your own identity. "With the best singers, you hear the first few bars of the song and the voice is unmistakable," says Carrie.

5. "In the last 50, we've got 15 to 20 singers who are better than almost anyone in the charts," says David. "Many pop stars can't cut it live. Especially with just a voice and piano, it's easy to spot an imposter."

6. If you've got a microphone, don't hold it up to your nose; hold it just under your chin so as not to obscure your lovely face. That's one of Uncle Mike's favourite tips.

7. "Some more developed voices have less character," says Carrie. "Someone who just sings in their bedroom can have loads of expression."

8. "If you make a mistake, your recovery rate has to be quick," says Carrie. "We might not notice your error, so just get on with the song."

9. "Always look in the mirror to practise your performance," says David. "Look for those wobbling heads, winking eyes, flappy arms… No, honest, they're flapping…"

10. Never drink fizzy or very cold drinks before you perform. They will cool down your warmed-up vocal chords. Foods to avoid are cheese and chocolate (they cause icky phlegm), and of course cigarettes are a no-no.

A STYLE DOCTOR WRITES

At this final stage of *Pop Idol*, choosing the right outfit can mean the difference between staying in the contest or being given the shove. Each week the show's stylist, Toni Porter, advises the contestants on what to wear. "Their image is extremely important now," says Toni, stylist to the stars. "They're wearing more raunchy, glamorous stuff and are starting to dress the way a pop idol would." Toni has some tips:

Choose something that's very distinctive and cutting edge. Sarah Whatmore's sheer gold outfit caught everybody's attention!

Think carefully about the whole outfit, as you want to make an impact.

Certain colours and patterns, such as small checks, stripes that are close together, and white, won't work on camera.

High-street clothes can look cheap on their own so mix them with a couple of more expensive items if you can.

Try out stuff you'd never normally wear as you may find it suits you.

Wear something quite different each week. It's important to keep updating your image.

Facing the press

It's not easy. They can be nice-looking, ugly, thin, fat, friendly or gruff. You can't tell the wily ones from the lovely ones. It's terrible but it's true. Most important is to forget what they appear to be like, and concentrate on what they're *asking* and what you're *replying*. Sentences can be taken out of context and words skewed, so make sure you are comfortable with what you're talking about. Here are the top six tips from the *Pop Idol* press office:

☆ Think about what may make a good/interesting story. Talk about things personal to you – anecdotes work really well.

☆ Do not give out personal phone numbers or addresses – if you are an interesting competitor, you or your Auntie Beryl may be hounded.

☆ It's your five minutes to impress and so use it to talk about you.

☆ Remember that you don't have to answer anything you're not comfortable with. Tell them so.

☆ The press want to help you – be polite and friendly and have fun! Go on.

☆ If you're asked about the judges, be honest, but remember that what you say may be in print before your audition!

A DOCTOR WRITES...

So, you want to be famous, but you're worried about going a bit wobbly? Celebrity shrink Beechy Colclough has "treated" Robbie Williams, Elton John and Michael Jackson. "People don't realise how tough fame can be," he says. "You need to be emotionally concrete to withstand the strain." Uh-oh. Let's read Beechy's list of showbiz tips on how to stay sane. If you want to, that is.

WHAT MIGHT HAPPEN:

☆ It will feel as if you are working a 25-hour day. You can't just shut down and switch off like most people do after work.

☆ **You're public property. You can't pick your nose and no one find out unless you are secured in a bunker.**

☆ Nobody will feel sorry for you when you moan about how hard it is. Nobody.

☆ **The temptation to turn to drugs and alcohol will be much greater. Yes.**

☆ Nobody will tell you how it is. You'll be surrounded by "yes" people who are all trying to protect you. It can make you precious and unable to cope when things do go wrong.

Tips to survive *Hello!* magazine

Don't forget to tidy up before they come round the house. A messy place is not very professional, is it? Better still, ring up an old pal like Lawrence Llewellyn Bowen and get him to do it for you.

Do mention all the charitable stuff you've been up to: saving the goat, planting runner beans for the ozone layer, etc.

Make sure to plug your new single, album, clothes-range at all times – don't talk about throwing up in a gumboot when you were five.

Borrow a friend's baby and look extra cute!

If they've asked about any recent holidays, pretend you've been out with Simon Cowell on an exotic beach adventure.

Er, on second thoughts, um… shall we start again?

HOW TO STAY SANE:

☆ **Spend time doing the things you used to do before you were famous. Bird watching or golf?**

☆ Sort your head out. See a therapist and sort out any emotional problems that might cause you problems later on in your career.

☆ **Walk down the street as if you are a nobody. Or at least with a hat on.**

☆ Don't forget where you came from. Buy yourself some postcards of your hometown and stick them in your wallet.

☆ **Remember, you're no better than anybody else out there. No, you're not. Even Brad Pitt says he makes sure he remembers that.**

☆ Make sure you have somebody in your life that you can be truly open with. The public eye is a lonely place to be. Get a parrot, or nick Geri Halliwell's dog.

A WORD FROM THE EXECUTIVE PRODUCER

The exec producer, ex-Mr Nasty Nigel, talks about the show, as he's been there every step of the way, out of the camera's view this time…

Has the programme been all you expected?

It's everything I hoped it would be when we started way back. I thought that having done the trawl before with *Popstars*, I would have got bored on the road this time, but I was intrigued to find more and more people coming forward. Then once we started getting the talent through – Will, Gareth, Sarah Whatmore – it was fantastic. We were anxious after the first few auditions, particularly one in London when we saw very little talent. We worried there weren't going to be enough people to choose from.

Everyone said 21 shows was too many, but what no-one realised was it's like three series in one. The initial stage of the auditions – the good, the bad and the cuddly – then the elimination process, then the performance part. It was never going to get boring. It hooked people along the way.

Simon upset a few people.

But he needed to be blunt. Sometimes kids waste their lives dreaming of being a pop star when they have little or no talent – it's stupid.

You had to tell Pete and Simon off when they argued with each other.

I think they went over the top. I was delighted for the TV channel, but once they started to hijack the show for their own pettiness and bickering the show steered off course. I wanted them to focus on the talent in front of them. I reprimanded them. Pete took it well and apologised, and Simon said, "B******" and put the phone down on me. He likes that word because he talks a lot of it.

Have you got emotionally involved?

It is highly charged, very emotional. I was wrapped up in it from day one. I am one of the few who see the phone-vote percentages and I'm amazed – it changes every week. The public is taking it all on performances, so it's not always the same person who wins. I'm delighted with that. They're not just getting on a bandwagon.

Ah.

The moment the Pop Idol is chosen, you're asking people to put their hands in their pockets to buy a record. The TV programme is over. It's, "This is my song, will you buy it?" It's not a 10p phone call – they've got to buy a CD.

11 become 2

And... we're down to the final ten. Throughout the week leading up to the first Big Saturday, the atmosphere is calm and jolly. Based in a smart hotel in north London, the ten go from press conference to photo shoot, health farm to Christmas shopping, then on to David and Carrie's for vocal training as if this is the most natural thing in the world. Aw, born pop stars... almost. The only problem is, our friend Rik.

THE SAGA OF RIK

Not everyone is feeling well for the first couple of weeks of the competition. Wintery flu and colds are being staved off with salads and water, though Aaron's preventative lager method is not taken up by all. Nice one, Aaron. Yet Rik finds he's in trouble – he can hardly talk, let alone sing – and it's doubtful he will make Saturday's show. There is much debate, especially in the newspapers, with some thinking he doesn't want to be in the competition. What, have Simon's high-waisted trousers really put you off, Rik???

The pressure Rik is under might have something to do with it, but he denies all of that. "When the germs take hold, they definitely take hold," he croaks. He is allowed a week off, after seeing a posh throatologist who confirms he is in big trouble, and mustn't even speak!

Yet the week after he is just as bad. Darius, who received the highest number of votes of the remaining contestants in his group, takes over. Rik is out... but ready to appear on *This Morning* a week later.

"I am gutted about not being in the show any more, but now I've got to pick myself up and concentrate on earning a living," says Rik. He's got plenty of offers of advice from top biz boffins and will probably be able to sign a deal with someone else, given all the attention he's had. Goodbye, Rik! Remember us all when you're a pop star!

THE FIRST ONE TO GO...

Nerves abound on the first Saturday night of the finals, and of course they would – what a big stage! What an audience! What a panel of judges! But again, no one is safe. This time, Laura is reduced to tears by Pete, who thinks she's a great performer with a chirpy personality but not a great singer. Pete falls in love with William, who sings Aretha Franklin, and Gareth is told to buck up and get competitive.

When it comes to the audience votes, the three lowest-scoring contestants have to sit on the "Couch of Cruelty". It's Laura, Korben and Jessica who perch there, wide-eyed, and hold hands together. And...

Gulp. Korben's out.

On TV the following Monday, he says he worries because of the press stories that were written the week before, that revealed he is gay. He wonders whether this influenced the phone votes. He still resolves to go on and be a Pop Idol, in any way he can. Good luck Korben!

This week, Darius is back, rehearsing along with everyone else. He looks happily bewildered with this unexpected turn of events.

HOW YOU VOTED: Will 27.3%; Gareth 26.3%; Zoe 10.8%; Rosie 10.5%; Aaron 6.8%; Hayley 6.8%; Jessica 4.6% Laura 4.3%; Korben 2.6%.

DARIUS'S (LONG) STORY

"It's been an incredible rollercoaster ten days. It all happened on the first week of the final ten. I got a call from the *Pop Idol* production crew. Would I be interested in standing in if someone falls ill on Thursday? I said I'd have to think about it because I'd closed the chapter on *Pop Idol* and was going to finish my degree.

"Production then rang and asked me to stand in on that Saturday. I found out that the number of votes on the week I didn't get through to the ten was as many if not more than some contestants now in the ten on other weeks. I felt that I could go back – if I hadn't had many votes, I wouldn't have felt I'd earned my place.

"Then production gave Rik another week to recover, so even though I had rehearsed a song, I didn't go on the first week. Each day of the following week had the newspapers carrying conflicting reports of Rik's health. Then I was woken on Wednesday by a phone call from one of the London radio stations saying, 'Congratulations! What song are you singing on Saturday?' I thought it was Aaron playing a prank on me. It wasn't. Then I open the *Sun* and Rik's dad is in it, saying nothing short of a Christmas miracle will bring Rik back. I was gutted for Rik, but over the moon to perform.

"Next production told me that Rik's dad planted the story in the *Sun*, without their permission, so I still wasn't definitely singing. I didn't sleep on Wednesday night, then finally on Thursday I got a phone call saying, 'Darius, we're really sorry to keep you waiting so long. You're singing on Saturday!'

"Suddenly I felt really privileged to be able to have a second chance. It's an incredible experience, performing to a live audience. There's a camaraderie amongst the ten. We boost each other along."

THE SECOND ONE TO GO...

The Christmas show is awash with festive cheer, and as Darius joins the gang everyone is steely. Someone's going to be voted out, and they've all got to do their best.

"Last week we all knew one of us was going to go," says Rosie, seriously, "but it doesn't make it any easier. You know someone's going to go every time... It could be you, or the person sitting next to you... It is very dramatised – that couch, it's a terrible thing! And it's a shame to see someone's dream dashed."

And yet this week, the well-praised Rosie is told by big fan Pete that she chose the wrong song, the saucy "Hey Santa!" William wears an ill-advised see-through shirt and manages to slow down "Winter Wonderland" to the utmost croonaway, smoothaway speed. Aaron's Elvis impersonation on "Blue Christmas" wows the grans.

The Couch of Cruelty invites Jessica once more, and Rosie, and Laura again. Blimey. They look a little stunned, but perhaps that's the effect of Dec's festive tie, which wouldn't look out of place on Lily Savage. And...

It's Jessica who receives the least votes this week and she's out on her ear. But who's this cheeky chappie come to give her a hug? It's Korben! Back this week to watch proceedings and provide moral support. Jess has got to go back to Wales for Christmas knowing she's not got through to next week, which will be hard, but her new-found friends cheer her up at the Christmas party after the show.

"Obviously I'm a bit gutted to be leaving," she says, "but I think my mum's more upset than I am. She's crying her eyes out!

"This has been the best experience of my life," she continues. "I'm so pleased to have got this far." And then she tries to find Pete Waterman to badger him for the millionth time about writing some songs for her...

HOW YOU VOTED: Will 22.6%; Gareth 20.8%; Darius 19%; Zoe 14.2%; Aaron 5.4%; Hayley 5.1%; Rosie 4.8%; Laura 4.3%; Jessica 3.8% .

THE THIRD ONE TO GO...

Post-Christmas but still looking svelte and adorable, the finalists are now down to eight. Hayley, in fact, has lost half a stone because she's been ill, poor lamb. She's trying to eat a bit more to put the weight back on. The gang have been doing a smart *OK!* magazine shoot this week and have been wearing some fancy gear. The trousers Rosie wears cost over £2,000! But she has to give them back at the end of the day. Everyone feels like a real Pop Idol, and relishes the attention.

On Saturday, nerves are nervier, tensions tenser. Today our friends are singing Burt Bacharach songs – most of which are notoriously hard to sing. Burt was no soft touch on the melody front. Laura gets a big thumbs-up for "Always Something There To Remind Me" and Hayley manages to wear little more than some undies and a net curtain. William is still proving popular. As Pete says, "The bad news is you're not a Pop Idol. The good news is you're a Superstar!"

Aaron doesn't fare so well. The judges don't think he quite cuts it – and the public isn't ready to vote him in for next week. Every one of the finalists looks miserable when they hear he has to go. They have all genuinely bonded with each other, and Aaron's been the one to keep everyone perked up with stupid jokes – and of course his catchphrase, "Spot on!" He is philosophical about his defeat.

"Someone has got to go," he says. "If it hadn't been me, it would still have been upsetting as I'm very close to all the contestants now." He admits, however, that he's surprised.

"I don't know what went wrong. I thought I did well – maybe the judges' comments went against me. It is a shame, but I won't give up. Being a pop star was my boyhood dream and now I've got this far, I can't turn back."

Jessica has turned up to cheer everyone on and slips into the green room after the show.

"It's horrible being in the audience," she says. "Because you know what it feels like to be booted off, you just can't bring yourself to clap when the loser is revealed."

Nigel Lythgoe says everyone was affected when Aaron was voted off.

"The atmosphere was strained after Saturday's show. Most of the production crew were feeling very glum as none of them wanted to see Aaron go. It seems he'd won a place in everyone's hearts.

"Pete called him 'the people's champion' and that's what he was. What you see is what you get with Aaron. There's no arrogance about him and everybody here has found him a pleasure to work with.

"However, he seemed out of his depth on Saturday night and the trouble is, he looked like a train driver from Newcastle and not a Pop Idol. I know it seems harsh, but you have to remember we are looking for a Pop Idol here and not just somebody with a fabulous voice."

HOW YOU VOTED: Will 21.3%; Gareth 21%; Darius 18.2%; Zoe 11.4%; Hayley 8.4%; Laura 7.1%; Rosie 6.9%; Aaron 5.7%.

THE FOURTH ONE TO GO...

Outside the Fountain TV studios in Wembley, north London, stands a group of girls, waiting near the gates, in the cold. Inside, seven Pop Idollers are rehearsing their songs to an empty studio, little knowing they have such dedicated fans. They've all been to Pete Waterman's studio this week to record the songs they're singing on Saturday, and they've loved it. They were stunned to see the amount of gold discs he has on his wall. "It's a reality day today," says Pete. "Some might find it the most frightening experience, some will take to it like ducks to water." He says everyone must perform 120 per cent, even though that's mathematically impossible.

Back at the studios there is a surprise in store. Caroline Buckley, better known as the "YMCA" girl, is back! She's been invited by the production team to sing after the show for the audience, and Carrie and David Grant are coaching her so she can hit the high notes of "Movin' On Up" by M People. And she ain't doing too bad... The finalists each go through their songs on the stage and they all encourage one another like they've been bosom buddies for years. William takes it upon himself to run up to anyone who needs a sip of water between rehearsals. What a sweet boy...

On Saturday, the atmosphere is again tense. "It really feels like people are missing now," says William. "The group is getting so small. I miss Aaron, he was so funny. I miss Jessica wittering away."

"It does get tenser," agrees Rosie, who's no stranger to the Couch of Cruelty. "You know every week you're going to get that awful feeling from the week before."

During the show, Gareth – still having his speech therapy – gets a good report from the judges, Hayley wows them all with "Show Me Heaven" and William is still doing 'mazin' soul, this time on "Ain't No Sunshine". Rosie and Laura – again – don't quite convince the judges.

At the end of voting, it's Zoe, Rosie and Laura who are on the couch, and it's Laura who makes her exit, emotionally.

"I expected to go," she says afterwards in the green room. "I've been preparing for this all week, so I knew it was going to happen. Zoe and Rosie can't stop crying, but I got all my crying done the first week I was on the couch. I really am fine about it." Pete Waterman comes into the green room to wish her well. "Everyone's been so supportive," continues Laura. "I'm really going to miss being in the show but when it's all over, I can hold my head up high."

The whole group gets very emotional, and Darius even asks Kate Thornton to stop filming for ITV2. "We've all grown very close so it's always sad when someone has to go," he says.

HOW YOU VOTED: Will 29.8%; Gareth 23.3%; Darius 18%; Hayley 10.8%; Zoe 7.8%; Rosie 5.5%; Laura 4.8%.

THE NEXT ONE DOWN...

This week has been luxurious, by all accounts, as the final six have been staying at Hanbury Manor health farm. However, their choreographer, Paul Roberts – he's worked with All Saints, Robbie and Atomic Kitten, to name but three – is putting them through their paces. Some are naturals when it comes to dancing – William and Zoe are clear leaders. Others, such as Rosie, who has not had any dance training before, are finding it difficult. Her legs hurt, she says. Darius is finding his immense height a little tricky – he's all limbs. Gareth is dumbfounded – he's never attempted anything like this before.

Fortunately, the health farm provides après-dance massage and everyone gets a bit of that. Zoe's hair straightens in the sauna and she has some new straight extensions put in. This, she says, took her mum over nine hours!

Gareth has everyone in stitches when he explains, quite seriously, his 2-2-1 hair formation. He creates two points in the front, two in the middle and one at the back. Not realising it's such a delicate operation, the others are completely taken aback. Gareth, they have discovered, always takes the longest to get ready, and now they know why.

"I thought Zoe was going to choke with laughter when we all heard that," says Hayley.

At rehearsals for Saturday's show the six are eating lunch in the studio canteen. And my, what a mess! Gareth is trying to put as many chips in his mouth as possible, aping his behaviour at Hanbury Manor, where he claims he tried to put a whole lobster claw in his mouth during a posh meal. Nice. He follows his light lunch with a healthy yoghurt... which he manages to ruin by dropping big bits of flapjack into, and eating both together. Zoe, a dainty eater by comparison, looks disgusted.

The six have now moved to an apartment together at the top of the hotel. Hayley is disappointed that she's not in her "lucky room" any more, but she's just as interested in Gareth's living habits.

"He is the tidiest one," she says. "There's no mess. But he has his S Club calendar hung by his jacket on the wall, and he has to have it at an angle because his jacket obscures the photo of Rachel. If you try to straighten it up he spots it and moves it back. He's very strange."

Gareth's mum has also been making her presence felt. She's been making Hayley cups of hot chocolate before she goes to bed and has provided Gareth with a big medicine box full of throat lozenges and cold remedies. Aw, Gareth, you little pampered thing, you.

Darius has been cooking for the others, and creating such delights as pasta and ice-cream. He made a three-course meal for all six, which they said was delicious. "But I think it just came out of jars," says Rosie. "It was lovely, though."

They love the apartment. "We just sit around in our pyjamas eating beans on toast," says Hayley. "It's nice to relax a bit more."

But all this is mere distraction, for Saturday's show is round the corner and it's rehearsal day today. William admits he feels less nervous as the series goes on, though he's not sure why. Rosie explains how she wouldn't have even entered the competition if it wasn't for her mum and her friends. She nearly pulled out of the Criterion auditions because she had so little self-belief, she admits. She's pleased to have more confidence now, but – and as everyone states time and time again – it's so difficult when people are knocked out.

It's Abba songs this week, and Pete Waterman thinks this round is hard. "Abba songs are the most difficult to sing." He should know – he's recorded Westlife singing one of them. This week does prove to be a bit sticky, with Rosie finding "Winner Takes It All" a bit of a struggle and Darius being told that "I Have A Dream" is a "girl's song" by Pete. Zoe and William get a good reception but Hayley thinks that generally the judges have been a bit harsh this time.

"They're hard songs. I think the judges could be a bit more understanding," she says.

When the phone lines are closed, the person with the least votes is Rosie. She looks steely and says what a good time she's had. Everyone else looks crestfallen because they'll miss their chum.

Then Pete bounds over and talks turkey. We all knew she was his favourite, but it looks like they're discussing a record deal. Pete is triumphant.

"She could be a superstar."

Rosie glows.

"I am really excited about the future," she says. "Of course, I'm disappointed that I'm not going through and I'm going to miss all my mates on the show, but there's no way I could go back to working in a shop now – I want to be a pop star."

HOW YOU VOTED: Gareth 36.6%; Will 25.2%; Zoe 14%; Darius 13.3%; Hayley 5.8%; Rosie 5.1%.

THE SIXTH ONE DOWN...

We are starting to enter the most terrifying weeks of the contest, viewers, as our remaining finalists – who have all bonded so well with each other – are fearing being voted off the programme… They also risk being parted from their new bestest pals; that's what they're finding the most difficult, it seems. Oh, they've been through so much together!

This week, everyone is extra-worried because they have to sing with a live band – this is a big test. When they go down to meet the boys at the studio, they crinkle with nerves. Hayley looks very ill indeed, as everyone has to get the feel for the swing rhythm and get some chemistry (man) with the trombonists. Everyone wants to prove that they're not just karaoke-style singers, that they really can croon to a live band, just like pop supremo Robbie Williams.

Vocal coach Carrie says Zoe is fearless, but David thinks she's not so certain where she's going. Zoe is singing "Get Happy", the song that Judy Garland made famous. Gareth has a few hiccups as he sings "Mack The Knife" like a Westlife record. "It's difficult for Gareth," says Carrie. "This shows up the weaknesses in his voice – he's got a pop voice."

Hayley is performing "That Old Devil Called Love". "She's got to use all the emotion in her voice," says David. She finds it tough at first, but soon gets into the swing (ha ha) of it. Will takes to it like a duck to water, singing "We Are In Love". David reckons he has a great voice. "In the end it was Will who was conducting the band. He's a forties' throwback!"

Darius finds it tricky getting the rhythm of swing, but soon he's as smoothalong as swing can get with "Let's Face The Music And Dance". What professionals, eh?

It's not just the singing – it's another hectic week just, well, existing. All five go back to their home towns. Gareth is mobbed at his school, with girls screaming their hearts out for him (he loved this: fact, fans!). Hayley returns to Birmingham to find the whole town rooting for her and a big sign saying "Vote Hayley" projected on a wall. Feeling the love in the, er, city, she weeps, "It makes me proud to be a Brummie!"

The famous five are starting to notice that they're getting just a little bit of attention wherever they go. At a film première during the week, they step out of their limo and the place goes mental. "We didn't think it was for us!" says Will. "We all looked around thinking, Who's just walked in?" A certain tabloid newspaper sets up a phone vote of its own during the week, and prints the results and the total votes each contestant gets. Would it be similar to the *Pop Idol* voting system? Have they let the cat out of the bag? No! Cos the newspaper got a few thousand votes and the TV programme gets a couple of million, and the numbers don't tally. But fame is a strange thing for the Pop Idols, and they don't really know how famous they are…

On Saturday, the show is sizzling. The audience – my goodness me – is completely hyped-up and roaring. The big band is certainly live, and fairly big. The Pop Idols are raring to go – they've been waiting for this moment all week. What an atmosphere.

All five sing their socks off and mightily impress the judges. "You are so sexy," Simon tells Hayley, but he thinks Darius has put in the weakest performance. And my, how Pete gets in a huff with this! He starts fuming and taking Simon to task because he thinks he has something against Darius.

"I have supported him throughout this competition," says Simon. "If we're not allowed to put an opinion over then what is the point of us being here?"

"I disagree," says Pete. "This is *Pop Idol*, not *Teen Idol*. I think age is an issue with you. You don't understand Darius. He sang the song as good as Nat King Cole. He was brilliant."

"Your problem is you get too emotionally involved," says Simon.

Ooh-er. But when it comes to the vote, the judges are all in agreement – their gut feeling is that Hayley could be off this week, but they say this grudgingly because, quite simply, everyone feels that all five were wonderful. Just marvellous.

When the phone lines close, the votes are counted, and it is Hayley who has to bow out gracefully this time. There have been 2.5 million – 2.5 million!!! – votes this week, a record breaker. Yet poor Hayley didn't quite get enough, even though she was brill.

"I never thought I'd get past the final ten. I really enjoyed it all," she whimpers, trying very hard not to blub on camera… but when Nicki Chapman and Kate Thornton come over to hug her afterwards they all start crying.

HOW YOU VOTED: Gareth 25.4%; Will 24%; Darius 23.7%; Zoe 15.6%; Hayley 11.3%.

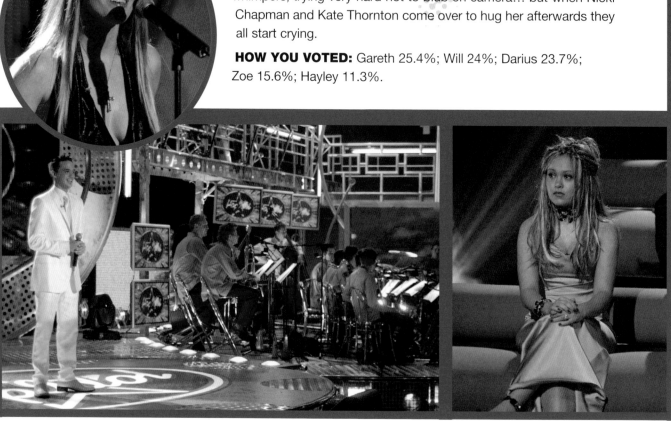

THE SEVENTH ONE DOWN...

With only four finalists left, emotions are high this week. Zoe, Gareth, Will and Darius rehearse the show for the final time on Saturday afternoon, and all their concentration is on the performance. There's no larking around, no comedy dancing – just true professionalism.

Everything has to be rehearsed, including the results show. Ant and Dec go through the end part, where a finalist is voted off.

Ant and Dec: "Will, sorry, mate, you got the lowest amount of votes, you'll have to go. Sorry. Have you enjoyed this week?"

Will: "Yes, it's been the best ever."

Ant and Dec: "Favourite day?"

Will: "My day off! It's been exhausting!"

Even at the rehearsal, the atmosphere is buzzing. Nigel Lythgoe wanders around, talking to Simon and Pete. It's like a pleasant coffee morning in a glamorous TV studio. Cheese and biscuits, anyone?

Surprisingly, even at this late stage, there's still no real rivalry between the contestants. They're closer than ever. There's no rivalry between the judges, either – no "Judge Idol" competitiveness. They watch the final four sing and rehearse their comments. Instead of saying, "Darius! You were marvellous!" they simply chat so they don't give anything away, asking if they know who wrote the song they're singing and what sort of week they've had. It's all so polite!

Yes, the judges bicker (Pete: "The people at home like these pearls of wisdom, Simon!"), but that's what we're used to. Otherwise, there's not a scandal in sight! If you could actually see scandals, that is.

The press have had a *Pop Idol* field day this week. Is it true that Zoe and Gareth are in a kiss-up situation? "No!" they both cry – they really are just very good friends.

"We got on together from the first day we met, but there's never been any romance," says Gareth.

The four have also dressed up as their pop idols for a newspaper. What you didn't see on TV was Will revealing in rehearsals why he chose Jamiroquai.

Simon: "You know Jay Kay hates the show?"

Will: "Yes. That's why I did it. I thought it would annoy him more."

Clever chap, Will, and highly controversial.

At a press conference, Darius was confronted with the fact that Britney has now seen the infamous clip of him singing "Baby One More Time", on *The Frank Skinner Show*.

"I just don't know how to respond to it," he says, looking blank.

Sitting in the audience this afternoon is Jessica, who's been back to watch every show so far. She's excited as she's just recorded a song that will be a

contender for the UK Eurovision entry. (Rumours that she's been asked to join Hear'say are unfounded.) She's also been ringing Pete to talk to him about recording, but hasn't had much luck so far. "He's a very busy man," she says. They've spoken today, but only about Jessica's Eurovision song.

Aaron was going to come along today, but Jessica reckons he's got another shop to open, so he can't. Hayley's coming down but she doesn't want to sit in the audience – as she's rooting for all four she fears she might get over-emotional when someone is voted out.

Kate Thornton is buzzing around. Since she mentioned on ITV2 that Pete's always rushing off to the loo, he's been sent some literature by a concerned medical society that deals with the, er, nether region side of things. Pete's given the letter to her, highly amused. Watching Zoe rehearse, Kate's knocked out. "She's got such a great voice," she says.

When it comes to the show, the audience is incredibly excited and people are on their feet even as the first titles roll. They're wilder than a pack of wolves who've just been handed free tickets to a Robbie Williams concert and a large plate of foxes to eat.

This week the four are singing Number One hits. Gareth sings Wham!'s "Wake Me Up Before You Go-Go" and the classic "Unchained Melody". The live band starts before he's ready as he goes into the second number, but he doesn't falter. Wow. He just starts the song and sounds amazing.

Darius sings "It's Not Unusual" by Tom Jones and "Whole Again" by Atomic Kitten. Natasha Kitten has come along specially, and she loves it. "You did a fantastic job. Well done!" she says.

Zoe performs Whitney's "I Wanna Dance With Somebody" and "The Power Of Love" by Jennifer Rush. Two forceful toons, yet she doesn't convince the judges, who believe she's being a little too ambitious. Will ends with The Eurythmics' "There Must Be An Angel" and The Bee Gees' "Night Fever". He gives it a lot of welly, that boy.

When it comes to the vote it's close. There's also a record amount of votes – 3.7 million!! Finally, Zoe – as predicted by the judges – has to go. Gareth starts crying immediately, and then everyone gets upset. Mum Tracey is close by to console her daughter, as everyone – including Jessica, Rosie and Hayley and members of the production team – gathers round for big hugs. Darnit, you can't say this lot aren't the best of friends. Fair brings a lump to your throat.

HOW YOU VOTED: Gareth 28.7%; Will 27.9%; Darius 24.5%; Zoe 18.9%.

THE EIGHTH ONE TO GO...

"I wasn't nervous before, ever, but I think I was in denial. This week, I just really want to get there, to the final."

William Young is sitting in the canteen of the TV Studio at Wembley and he's looking very tired, but there's still a fire in his eyes. It's been a bit of a week, and no one's had enough sleep. On Sunday the boys each record a version of the double-A-side single, Westlife's "Evergreen" and "Anything Is Possible" by Cathy Dennis. They all find it nerve-wracking at first, in front of a mic, not an audience – Darius has to sing slightly higher than he's used to, to keep the song in the same key, but after a bit of reassurance he knows he can do it. Simon pops down to give some support, and the results are... incredible. "If it's not a number one hit I'm going to eat my very high-waisted trousers," says Simon. In his office on Friday he plays the Gareth track, and he beams with excitement.

Not only that, but the three boys were off to Dublin on Wednesday to sing at the S Club 7 gig. They were blown away, they were. There was an audience of 7,000 and they were all screaming their heads off for the P'Idols and Will, Gareth and Darius absolutely adored the experience.

"The wall of sound hit me when I went on," says Darius. "It was the most incredible thing, seeing that sea of people, glow-sticks waving and from the crowd the sound of people singing." Darius shakes a lot afterwards, poor chap.

"I loved it, it was amazing," says Gareth. He can't stop grinning afterwards.

"It was completely different to the show, different than singing into a camera," says Will. Rachel is raving about him. "Absolutely amazing," she says. They all admit it really felt like they were Pop Idols tonight, and it will be strange going back to the competition on Saturday. They want to be set free! Ah, but not yet...

On Saturday the three are very focussed. This is a big night, and nerves are high. Everyone is fussing back stage, getting ready and warming up.

The three boys are such good friends now; Will and Gareth really bonding and being silly together. The flat's a mess this week, the washing-up has certainly not been done. Darius hasn't even had much time to cook up his wonderful meals.

"I don't think that Gareth has done the washing-up very often, if you see what I mean," says Darius. But now now, you've all got some songs to sing...

The judges have picked the songs this week, and Gareth sings "Yesterday" and "Flying Without Wings". His swoonaway versions of the song go down really well with the judges. Will sings "Sweetest Feeling" and "Beyond The Sea", and the judges love his voice as well. Darius sings "Make It Easy On Yourself" and "Dancing In The Moonlight". The judges go crazy for young Darius! Golly, they're very tender-hearted these days, eh?

By the end of the show, 5.8 million votes have come in, which is amazing. This programme is only the biggest TV talent search ever, you know. It's very close, but Darius just misses the final show by getting 21% of the vote (1.2 million: figures, fans!). He may well be the most resilient man in the world, the self-styled "happiest boy in Britain", for he does not crumble, he just has to cradle

his wee brother who seems more upset than he is. Darius thanks "everybody that picked up a telephone and made my dreams come true" and continues, "This is not the end, this is just the beginning." Oh yes.

"I think Will or Gareth will make the most incredible Pop Idol," says Darius a little later. "I think they're both fantastic. I've no regrets about coming on this show." Simon Fuller, the programme's creator, spends the rest of the time fielding calls from record companies interested in signing Darius…

Nicki is very supportive. "I think Darius has got a fantastic future. When he left *Popstars* it was a different Darius – the media was on his back, but tonight he got respect from every person in the country. He's a true artist, a fantastic performer. I am so proud, out of everybody, he has made the furthest journey, he turned it round for himself and the general public."

But relax not, viewer! Now things are getting really sticky – next week is going to be massive. Will and Gareth are as close as close can be in the nation's popularity stakes. One of them received 39.8% of the vote, and the other received 39.3!!! Only 29,000 votes in it, which ain't many – a fight to the finish.

Will says about Gareth: "We keep looking at each other, going waaaaahhh! I feel like screaming!"

Blimey, even *The Official Pop Idol Book* feels wobbly…

HOW YOU VOTED: Will 39.8%; Gareth 39.3%; Darius 20.9%.

POP IDOL FACT!

Simon Cowell bit into his apple while talking to Darius in the recording studio and then… choked!

POP IDOL FACT!

The papers have said that Will's parents have been blasted by Gareth's mum, for not dancing along with everyone else during the programme's recording. "It's not true! My mum says you can see them dancing on the telly!!" Gareth says his mum didn't say it and has been upset since the story got out. Tut tut, newspapers.

POP IDOL FACT!

Gareth's "old flame" was featured in the Sun newspaper and said they'd met at a talent contest and he's sent her lots of saucy text messages. Gareth says he doesn't know her at all! "It's all lies, lies, lies," he says. She reckons she looks like Zoe, the paper says. "No way!" says Gareth.

POP IDOL QUOTE!

Darius gets a card from some nurses who are big fans. They work in a psychiatric hospital. Darius says, "Oh thank you! If I ever go nuts I know where to go…"

POP IDOL FACTS!

ROSIE RECORD DEAL

Pete did not offer Rosie a deal last week. "She just knows she's got a job at PWL if she wants one," he says. "I've not made an official offer." Still, bet she'll take him up on it soon.

POP IDOL FACT!

Nigel Lythgoe is getting emotionally involved.

"This one's been one of the most emotional so far. The production crew was in tears when they heard Zoe was going, as everybody adores her."

NIGEL'S VIEW

"What were Pete and Simon going on about this week? As the executive producer of the programme, I will have to reprimand both of them. I am sick of listening to their petty arguments. They need to realise that this show is not about them but about the talent in front of them. Simon is of course allowed his opinion, and Pete is allowed to disagree with it, but they're turning into a slightly senile, bickering old couple that didn't have the courage to get divorced 20 years ago."

POP IDOL FACT!

Kate Thornton questions Simon about the press article he was featured in, where he said he thinks Gareth is going to win.

"As a judge, should you have said that?" she asks.

"Probably not, no," he replies.

"Naughty boy!" says Kate.

POP IDOL FACT!

The final ten are allowed to come back and watch the show if they've been voted off. Korben even arrived with Helen Farrar from the final 50 last week.

POP IDOL FACT!

Hayley's still staying in the Pop Idol flat, and Zoe's not going home now either.

"I've been in the flat ever since I was voted off," says Hayley. "It's weird being there when you're not taking part in the show, but I've enjoyed myself. I'm not ready to go home yet and I want to be around for Zoe because I know exactly how she feels."

S CLUB LOVE POP IDOL

Voice coach Carrie Grant says, "I'm working with S Club 7 at the moment and they all love the show. Victoria Beckham also watches it and is a big fan of Will Young." Burlimey.

Carrie has worked with bands such as Take That and the Spice Girls, yet she lurves the Pop Idol finalists to bits. "David and I have been blown away by the level of talent. We didn't expect to find such amazing singers."

Summing up

Pete WATERMAN

Has being a judge on Pop Idol been what you expected?

Yeah, pretty well. I think that the talent has grown in stature as the show has gone on. It's been a long period, three months. They've been working with professionals so if they hadn't improved, there'd be something wrong.

And the public response?

Above what I expected, absolutely phenomenal. I expected it to be successful, but it's gone beyond that. Everybody I speak to, all they want to talk about is *Pop Idol*. People talk to me about Simon, and ask why don't I bash him on the show. I say, "Not on TV. I'll wait for the series to end first."

On screen, you did have a barney with Simon...

More than that – the show got very heated at times off screen, nothing to what you saw on screen. Simon is passionate about the show, particularly about his view of who should win, and I don't agree. I think it's down to the public. I don't believe judges should guide the public vote, saying, "You are the Pop Idol." That says that no one else in the show has a chance. If Darius wasn't good, he wouldn't have been in the last five. You can't say, "You shouldn't be here." Darius has built up his votes and upset everything – nobody thought Darius would be in at this stage. I like that – he's the joker, he's upset all the voting.

Simon said you were getting too emotionally involved...

Don't fall for that line. Simon is just trying to be a smartarse. Simon is far more involved than me. I ain't telling you to vote for anybody, I'm giving comments as an expert. I have not said at any time on the show, "You will win this competition," and we have all heard that constantly, every time Gareth walked through the door. I really don't think the winner is a foregone conclusion. The Saturday night final will be an amazing vote. I don't think you can call it. Simon thinks he can call it. People will vote for the winner.

What can you predict for the winner?

I can't predict anything – I'm only a judge. That's Simon and Nicki's job. My job finishes on Saturday night. I won't produce the winner. I won't get involved with any artists unless I feel nobody else wants to. Darius, Will or Gareth, I certainly wouldn't work with them in the current situation. Perhaps next year, but not while they're still in the throes of the cameras, being filmed everywhere.

What's the best rumour you've heard about the show?

The great thing is I was famous before, and I heard rumours about me that make Simon's love life sound boring. People always come up with half-baked stories, but I don't read the papers.

Have you spoken to Jessica about a deal?

I'm not taking any calls until after the show finishes. That's what a professional judge should do.

Have you been in touch with the final ten?

I find the sad thing about the industry is you never make friends, you make acquaintances. I can count my friends on one hand. If we've touched the final 50's lives for a brief time... If they remember us I'd be flattered, if not I wouldn't be insulted. In a year's time, they may want to forget they were ever on the show.

What's happening with Rosie?

I still don't know where we are. I have to wait to see what the show decides to do with her. She's still under contract with *Pop Idol* for three months after the show ends.

Nicki CHAPMAN

Has this been what you expected?

Yes, but much more fun. I had a taste before with *Popstars*, but this has been absolutely amazing. The public vote has made a huge difference and the standard coming through the door has been higher. We saw 10,000, compared to 1,200 for *Popstars*.

What about the public response?

People were more cynical with *Popstars*, but on *Pop Idol* the public does respect the judges, and they respect the contestants more. We knew the TV audience would like it, but we had no idea how much. People want to be involved, they'd like to be a judge, to become an A&R person. I did *This Morning* today, and there was Fern telling me afterwards that she doesn't go out on Saturdays, she loves the show. The audience is across the board, from kids to 70-year-olds. Everyone has an opinion.

What are your personal highlights?

Getting to the top ten and seeing ten amazing people. There wasn't really anyone who shouldn't have been there. Seeing 10,000 meant we could see a whole range of people, who we might not necessarily meet otherwise, someone like Will. The competition really has seen him make such improvements and glow.

Have the judges ever really fallen out over anything?

We've fallen out, but everybody remains friends. Certainly when we were on the road, you only saw a snippet of what went on. I have this "Nice Nicki" tag, but don't get me wrong, I'm no pushover. Any person I've worked with would tell you a different story. I'd say I was diplomatic.

What do you predict for the winner?

Huge success, a whirlwind – and continued success. They will get to perform great music, and that's the key. The general public put them there – let's hope they support them after.

Do you hang out with the last ten?

I see them more than the rest of the judges. I go up and have talks with them all. I can't disclose what they're about! Contract things, topics varying, across the board: video, press, promotion. I don't hang out with them; that's not what it's all about for me. They have their friends and family for that.

Could you have predicted the last five?

Within reason, yes. It's easy to say that now, but I did have a good idea.

Do the judges' opinions influence the vote?

I think it helps. The public does respect what we have to say, but they might not agree. They might think, "He's a sod, but he's right."

Best rumour you've heard about the show?

That we paid Rik to leave. Ludicrous.

Dr FOX

Has being a Pop Idol judge been what you expected?

Ooh, way more than that. It's been so much fun, very emotional and very inspiring. I knew it was going to be fun, cos I've been friends with Simon for long time and I knew Pete and Nicki a little. Originally we weren't going to be featured throughout the whole series, but just make appearances here and there after we'd chosen the final 50 and at the very end, but our characters worked so well together, we were part of the entertainment mix.

Has Simon been portrayed as a real baddy by the press? You knew him before...

In most cases I don't think Simon comes across as nasty, he's just really honest. Anyone sitting at home would agree with him, apart from the families of the people involved, but he has gone too far a couple of times. I lost my rag with him when he turned into a bit of a bully. You have to stop short of sticking the knife in, it doesn't achieve anything. What I said was all completely genuine and unrehearsed. He laid into little Oliver Manson in the heats – who, to be honest, gave a dreadful performance – but what he said was uncalled for, 'If you get through we're not doing our job properly.' It's meant to be a positive show, it's not about being a w*****.

Are you happy with your profile?

Earlier on, the TV critics made malicious remarks because they were green with envy; they were desperate to be sitting on that sofa judging a show like this. I've been in the business a long time and I can take it on the chin. Most of it made me smile. The press hasn't been digging into my personal life, just Simon's – and he leads, er, a different lifestyle from the rest of us. But if we're bold enough to criticise other people then we have to be able to take criticism too. I am really happy about the way I've come across on screen. I am fair and I am honest and that is what people have seen me to be.

Your dress sense has calmed down since starting the show...

I did wear a pink shirt once. It looked awful and I got a lot of stick in the press – deservedly – and enough flack from the other judges. I've been a loud-shirt man, but sitting there on an important TV show, that wouldn't be the right thing to wear. I'm 40 years old now.

Have Pete and Simon really fallen out?

Those two are like a couple of old battleaxes. They sit there and bitch at each other but they've been mates for about 20 years and they soon get over it.

Will you be forced to play the Pop Idol's records on radio – even if you don't like them?

I'll get the records first because I'm part of the show but the reality is that Simon Cowell and Simon Fuller are pop music geniuses – there's no point in them putting out a song I couldn't play on the radio. The single is incredibly radio friendly and will be hammered to death by every station, I'm sure. It will probably sell half a million in the first week.

Best rumour you've heard about the show?

That the whole thing was rigged from the start. It can't be rigged, quite simply, the TV watchdogs and phone watchdogs are looking at it too closely. We put our favourite 50 in, perhaps the things we said may have had an effect on the voting, but the public voted in the end.

Simon COWELL

Has being a judge on Pop Idol been what you expected?

We knew we needed a very strong panel and a variety of opinions. Apart from the odd conversation I had with people individually, we only met as a group the night before the first audition in Manchester. I said to the other three, "I think there's only one way to approach this, and that is, we have to be honest every time we give an opinion, and if we disagree with each other we have to say that as well." Whether there's a camera there or not, if I don't like something – whether I'm right or wrong – I've always got an opinion. We had 10,000 people to get through, so we've got to be like a hot knife through butter.

You never felt you were a little harsh on the auditionees?

You can't think about that. If you were making a judgement on a one-by-one basis as to whether they could handle rejection or not, these auditions would have lasted six years.

What's been most difficult?

The early stage was the easiest part to judge for me, because when someone came in and couldn't sing a note, it was easy to say to them, "You can't sing." When you get to the later part of the competition it becomes more difficult to give a proper assessment, because when you've got down to the last five you know these people. Anyone who's got into the final five deserves to be there unless they completely cock up on the night. That can happen – when we were down to the final six Rosie totally and utterly blew it. My God, that girl can sing, and if she cocked up, anyone can. I think, to be honest, if I went for one of them now I would be assassinated. It's self-preservation at this point.

What's been your highlight?

We'd normally expect to do well with six-and-a-half million viewers but now we've gone over 11 million. As we sit here it feels bigger than the general election. Shows you what a boring lot politicians are at the moment.

Have the judges ever really fallen out over anything?

There were two moments, both directed at me, one where Foxy had obviously bottled something up for weeks and just let it out. I looked into his eyes and he was not amused. Pete was a different kind of being annoyed. He just snapped and I didn't mind that in the slightest. 90 per cent of the conversations I have with Pete Waterman end in an argument, but we've never let it affect our working relationship. He's a very passionate man and we are both emotionally involved.

Are you comfortable with your new high-profile persona?

You have to ignore the tags that are put on you – Nasty Simon, Cynical Simon, all that. It's irrelevant. You have to look at it in two ways – how it's affecting your personal life and how it's affecting your business life. Personally, my friends think it's just fun so it doesn't make any difference. Professionally, I think it's going to help because if you are well known for speaking your mind, hopefully when you find people with an extra talent they'll like the idea of being signed up by you.

And your advice if someone reading this book is going on holiday and the tabloids are going to follow them around?

Very simply, don't take yourself too seriously. We knew we had a controversial show and that's the only reason the papers were interested in photographing me on holiday.

Are you on good terms with the final ten? Do you hang out with them?

I've always tried to make a point of not talking to the contestants before we comment, because it puts you in a very difficult position. It's unfair of me if I see them in rehearsals and think to myself, "You could be out this week," then jolly up with them beforehand and then lay into them. I talk to them afterwards, but I have to be slightly distant.

It's obvious your favourite has always been Gareth...

But I was the first person who criticised him, seven or eight weeks ago when he gave a weak performance, and the others agreed. Once he got his act together from the Abba show onwards, I thought he was brilliant. At the end of the day you have to do this job as a human being, and if you think one person is better than the others you have to say it.

Is it hard to lighten up?

I found the last two weeks very stressful. I think we all took it a bit too seriously at one point. I was sitting thinking that I was nervous about what I was going to say – not because of the way the public was going to perceive me but because one of the three judges was going to jump down my throat. Then I thought, "F*** it, if they want to have a go at me, they should have a go at me."

Have you had much hate mail?

For every ten letters that come in, only one is ever horrible, and the horrible ones are hilarious: "How dare you be on TV???"

What happened with Rik?

I think we made the right decision with Rik – that he had to go in the end. I think he imploded. I felt very sorry for him when he came in humble, broken almost: "You're going to kick me out but I proved to you that I can sing." We argued publicly but he got through, then he blew it by showing a side of his personality the public will never like, which is ego. You know you always get the best information from the make-up artists, and they were the ones who alerted me to Rik.

What advice do you have for the winner?

Don't believe the hype. The idiot Craig who won *Big Brother* told everyone he had signed a five-album deal, which was complete nonsense. You have to understand why you're here, who made you, and keep your feet on the ground. As much as people want you to succeed, there's going to be a huge amount of people that want you to fail. That puts pressure on everyone, so it's all about quality control now.

The Grand Final

WILL

Do you feel famous yet?

Yes, I do now, I think. I had a letter from a lady in prison – a lovely letter, sensitive, intelligently written. She didn't ask for anything, she just said, "I want to say that I can't get to a phone 'cos they won't let us vote, but if I could I would." I felt then that you can really touch people. It sounds so cheesy to say but she was someone much more isolated than most of the public. I really felt like the show was getting through all these barriers, even getting through the walls of the prison. I was so touched I had to write back immediately.

Do you feel different to how you did when you started?

Not as a person. I feel like a singer and I can say to people now that I'm a singer. I'd never have said that before because I'd think people's eyes would just glaze over and they'd just say, "Riiiight." They presume so much about you.

Is it different now there's only two of you?

I do feel the absence of everyone else. You look around and think, Is that it? We fit in the back seat of a car – before it took two people carriers. Gareth and I have really bonded over the past couple of weeks. We're not competitive.

WILL'S MANIFESTO

I pledge to stay true to myself and my beliefs at all times.

I pledge not to become a music-industry diva and not to request lychees on tap 24/7.

I pledge to stay away from typical celebrity hangouts.

I pledge not to throw celebrity strops at stalker journalists and paparazzi (I reserve the right to break this pledge).

I pledge not to wear my trousers at an unacceptable waist height.

I pledge to respect and entertain my fans at all times.

Have you had time to keep up your diary?

I haven't done my diary for a long time but it's a thing I write if I'm in the mood. I had to write an article for the *Sun* a week ago and they sent it back 'cos they said it was too intellectual! I thought it was funny, really hysterical, but I always do with my own writing. I really want to write an interesting perspective on *Pop Idol* for the broadsheets once it's over.

Who's impressed you most during your Pop Idol time?

Darius. I still don't understand him fully as a person, I just respect him for coming back in the public eye after making such a prat of himself. I really respect Gareth. I never thought about his stutter being so difficult for him, and never thought we were similar as people, but now I think we could remain friends after the show. There's six years' difference between us.

How do you feel the judges are reacting now?

They were pretty unimpressed by my performance two weeks ago when I sang "Night Fever" and "There Must Be An Angel". I wish I'd said something back now. I felt passionate about it. They were two very different songs and I thought I'd tried my best.

Are you nervous about Saturday?

No, not nervous, it's just so exciting – we're both really excited.

GARETH

Do you feel famous yet?

The Dublin concert was the only real time I felt like I was famous. People were screaming my name – to have that was just, wow!

Do you feel different to how you did when you started?

I was speaking to my friends and they said I've changed so much. When they say that, they don't mean it's for the worse, it's for the better. I've become a lot more confident and independent. I've only just started to live my adult life, so it's kind of strange. I don't feel a world away. I always said I will keep my feet on the ground, always.

Have you had any rude propositions from fans?

I've had women write to me – "I want to have your babies" and stuff. No, I haven't gone for that yet. One woman – I don't know how old she was – she lifted up her top and said, "Will you sign these?" I just walked off. She had a bra on underneath but I was like, What you doing? The amount of fan mail is unbelievable – I can't read all of it at once. Every letter I get I send them back a signed photo, which at the moment is costing so much! So many people don't know where I live, but they address the envelope to "Gareth Gates, Bradford, Pop Idol" and it gets there. I get about 120 letters a week.

Who have you been most impressed by during your Pop Idol time?

The two people I think are amazing are Ant and Dec 'cos they're really funny, really down to earth.

Did you feel embarrassed at crying on live TV?

It's just one of those things. If I was able to help it I wouldn't have cried but I couldn't hide my feelings. The hardest thing for me in the competition has already happened – having to say goodbye to Zoe.

Have your table manners improved?

I think they're getting better, too.

How do you feel the judges are reacting now?
I didn't know that Pete was at loggerheads with Simon about me. Really, I have to stay focused on the performance.

Personal highlight?

My highlight up until Wednesday night was getting 62 per cent in the heats. Now it's Dublin – the reason why we're all here is because we'd love to perform to thousands. It's really strange because you're there, and you're on stage and you have this awesome feeling inside you, because on the shows you're performing to nine million but you can't see them. It was amazing. I loved it.

Are you nervous about Saturday?

I'm usually nervous when I'm waiting to go on, but not awful nerves, not throwing up. It's half nerves and half excitement. Once I'm on stage it just goes and I really enjoy it. When we started off we were all really nervous, and the more we do it, the less nervous we are, although the more we do it, the less people are left.

GARETH'S MANIFESTO

I pledge not to throw celebrity strops or become a high-maintenance pop star.

I pledge to retain the 2-2-1 formation (hairstyle) for as long as possible.

I pledge not to give photo shoots in posh mansions claiming they are my home.

I pledge to work hard and give my fans everything they deserve.

I pledge not to become a celebrity bighead and vow to keep my feet firmly on the ground.

I pledge not to accept lavish gifts from other celebrities in a bid for publicity.

The big night

In the past 15 weeks, the contestants have never discussed the elimination process; apart from one time at Hanbury Manor Health Farm. This last week is no different – Will and Gareth have got extremely close and they concentrate on their performance rather than that tricky bit at the end of the show…

On finals night, the atmosphere is electric.

At first, it's only the final ten that are screaming. As they walk in during rehearsals and meet up in the studio canteen, they shout and holler, hugging each other and jumping about. "Zoe!" "Rosie!" "Hayley!" "Aaron!" They'll be in the audience tonight and on stage at the results show.

The show has reached epic proportions – questions were asked following Will and Gareth's "Battle of The Buses" on dad-friendly TV-debate programme *Any Questions?* The political voting process seems dull in comparison to *Pop Idol*'s glittering bus-led campaign. Gareth and Will have been on the road all week in their specially branded buses, talking to their public and completing almost 100 interviews. Debate has raged – can Gareth sustain his popularity? Where will Darius's portion of votes go? And who is the Queen voting for? Celebrity *Pop Idol* fans are numerous – Noel Gallagher watches every week and backs Gareth; Posh and Becks are gunning for Will. Robbie Williams is a Will fan but Natasha from Atomic Kitten favours Gareth.

Tonight, even the top celebs have turned up to watch the show live. Tamsin Outhwaite is sitting in the canteen with a furry hat on, giving Kate Thornton a good-luck present. Charlotte Church is another one in a hat, standing quietly in the corner. Lisa ex-from Steps is looking tanned, talking to Brian from *SM:TV* live. Comedians Sean Hughes and Ricky Gervais are looking jolly, sitting round a table which is host to many a beer bottle. Who do they think will win?

"GARETH!!" they chime.

High-octane stars, yes, but also high-octane murmurings: Gareth's mum chats away to 19 Management and Darius and Simon Cowell huddle up in a corner. Rumours of record deals already being signed are rife; can it be true that Will's recorded "Light My Fire" already? That Gareth and Will are already signed to BMG and that Burt

Bacharach is writing songs in LA for Will as we speak?

ARGH! We don't know!!

The only rumour we can confirm is that yes, the studio nearly burnt down at rehearsals: during Will's "Light My Fire" the real-live flames caught one of the cameras!

As the show starts, and the hollering and screaming kicks in, it feels like the Biggest Show On Earth, and it is. Will sings "Light My Fire" and the double a-sides of the first single: "Anything Is Possible" and "Evergreen". Gareth sings "Unchained Melody" and the two songs from the single. Both look like superstars – Gareth in ultrabrite white and Will in smouldering (if he gets too near those flames again) navy. They have loved this week so much, become firm friends and are just excited to be here at the final. Aw. Will they stay so grounded when they're superstars? Er…

The judges, in posh dinner jackets, are blown away. Simon calls Gareth a "pop idol" and Will a "superstar". But it's the public vote that counts, and over the next hour or so nearly nine million votes come in. NINE MILLION!!!! And the vote, ooh, it's so close! One of the boys got 53.1%, the other 46.9%… and the winner is…

WILL!

The place erupts; the whole production crew break down in tears and Will and Gareth look completely speechless. Will is delighted, Gareth is delighted for Will. Everyone wants to ask them questions, but they just want to be with their families and take it all in. The last word will have to rest with our comedian buddies, Ricky and Sean, still surrounded by beer, still excitely frothing about the competition.

"We told you Will would win, we said so."

Er, are you sure? Didn't you mention Gareth??

"No! Will! It was Will!" And with that, the celebs, the winners and their families party into the night; as the pop chart shudders in its bed with the thought of a few years of frenzied activity from the 'mazin talent this show has discovered… they'll all be back, you just watch 'em.

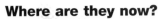

Where are they now?

Laura is advertising sofas and will be presenting on Nickelodeon in April.

Hayley's reporting on the Brits for *This Morning* and may do more presenting for them.

Zoe is weighing up record company offers.

Aaron's singing on a charity single with Cliff and will sign to a major record company.

Jessica is singing one of the UK entrants for the Eurovision Song Contest 2002.

Rosie has yet to hear from Pete Waterman…

Darius is weighing up record company offers.

Korben is waiting to get the right offer, he's back selling mobile phones.